Walt Whitman

Walt Whitman

BY CATHERINE REEF

ILLUSTRATED WITH PHOTOGRAPHS AND PRINTS

CLARION BOOKS

New York

Clarion Books

a Houghton Mifflin Company imprint

215 Park Avenue South, New York, NY 10003

Text copyright © 1995 by Catherine Reef

Type is 13.5/16 Bembo

Book design by Carol Goldenberg

Library of Congress Cataloging-in-Publication Data

Reef, Catherine.

Walt Whitman / by Catherine Reef.

p.   cm.

Includes bibliographical references (pp. 139–140) and index.

ISBN 0-395-68705-5

1. Whitman, Walt, 1819–1892—Biography—Juvenile
literature.   2. Poets, American—19th century—Biography—
Juvenile literature.   [1. Whitman, Walt, 1819–1892.   2.
Poets, American.]   I. Title.

PS3232.R44   1995

811′.3—dc20

[B]   94-7405
                                                                       CIP
                                                                       AC

HOR 10 9 8 7 6 5 4 3 2 1

*Frontispiece: The engraved portrait of Walt Whitman
that appeared in the first edition of* Leaves of Grass.

For my husband, John,
and my son, John Stephen.

Contents

Walt Whitman

Walt Whitman in 1853.

CHAPTER ONE

The Flood-Tide

I am with you, you men and women of a generation,
or ever so many generations hence . . .

*I*N THE LAST half hour before darkness, long rays of sunlight stretched across New York's East River. The sunset shone gold on a flock of seagulls wheeling in the sky. Beneath the birds, the Fulton Ferry chugged out onto the water. It moved away from Manhattan, a crowded island hemmed in by the masts of sailing ships. The ferry headed across the river toward the growing community of Brooklyn.

Within the crowd of passengers on that December day in 1855 stood a man dressed in laborer's clothes. In his checkered shirt, baggy pants, and broad-brimmed hat, Walt Whitman resembled the crew that piloted the ferry. He had the large build and ruddy face of someone who spent his time outdoors.

Whitman admired the simple, hardworking ferryboat pilots. He often rode beside them on his many trips across the river. I am a common working man too, his clothes told the world. But Whitman's own work was anything but common. Walt Whitman, a former journalist, teacher, and builder, had chosen to be a poet.

The poems in Whitman's small book, *Leaves of Grass*, expressed how it felt to be one man, yet one with all humanity. "Every atom belonging to me as good belongs to you," he told his readers. Whit-

1

man's poetry proclaimed his love for his fellow human beings. Through his words, Whitman believed, he could reach across time and great distances to connect with other people. The poetry in *Leaves of Grass* spoke directly to its readers, asking them to "[thrust] me beneath your clothing, / Where I may feel the throbs of your heart or rest upon your hip . . ."

Walt Whitman found inspiration all around him. He wrote about the people he saw on his walks through New York City. He described the beaches of Long Island, where he was born, as well as that "Howler and scooper of storms," the sea. He celebrated the human body and explored his own complex human soul. "What a history is folded, folded inward and inward again," he wrote, "in the single word I."

Today, the ferry ride inspired Whitman's imagination. He leaned against the rail and focused his pale eyes on the islands in New York Bay. He saw ships entering the harbor, ships flying the flags of far-off lands. A chilly wind rustled his gray beard as he turned toward the foundries on Brooklyn's shore. There, workers poured molten metal into molds to form tools and machine parts. In the twilight, their fires reflected yellow and red on the roofs of nearby houses.

As he looked on these familiar scenes, Whitman thought about the many people who had also looked upon them. He thought about the many others, people not yet born, who would do so in the future. One hundred years later, those ferryboat passengers would share Whitman's experiences on that winter day. Whitman wrote:

> Others will enter the gates of the ferry and cross from shore to shore . . .
> . . . .
> Others will see the shipping of Manhattan north and west, and
>   the heights of Brooklyn to the south and east,
> Others will see the islands large and small . . .

Whitman used his poem to speak directly to the future ferry riders, and to tell them he shared their feelings:

Vessels lined up along Manhattan's waterfront in the 1800s, while sailing ships, steamboats, and ferries navigated the East River.

I am with you, you men and women of a generation, or ever so
      many generations hence,
Just as you feel when you look on the river and sky, so I felt,
Just as any of you is one of a living crowd, I was one of a crowd,
Just as you are refresh'd by the gladness of the river and the
      bright flow, I was refresh'd . . .

He watched the incoming tide, the "flood-tide," creating a strong current in the river. Whitman imagined himself to be part of another flood tide, the steady current of time. It was a "current rushing so swiftly and swimming with me far away," he noted. All people, past, present, and future, were caught in the great flood tide of time. "Just as you stand and lean on the rail, yet hurry with the swift current," Whitman told his future readers, "I stood yet was hurried."

The poet included these lines in a poem titled "Crossing Brooklyn Ferry." He added the poem to a new and larger edition of *Leaves of Grass*, published in 1856. Whitman continually added new poems to *Leaves of Grass* and revised his old ones. By the time he published the final edition, in 1892, the slim book that contained twelve poems in 1855 had grown into a hefty collection of nearly four hundred poems. As an old man, Whitman called *Leaves of Grass* his "reason-for-being." It was, he said, his "life comfort."

Walt Whitman lived at a time when industry and immigration caused America's cities to grow rapidly. He described the bustle of nineteenth-century city life and the "Sounds of the city":

> *. . . the loud laugh of work-people at their meals . . .*
> *. . . . .*
> *The heave'e'yo of stevedores unlading ships by the wharves,*
> *   the refrain of the anchor-lifters,*
> *The ring of alarm-bells, the cry of fire, the whirr of swift-*
> *   streaking engines and hose carts . . .*

It was the century when pioneers moved west and railroads first crossed the Great Plains. "I hear the locomotives rushing and roaring, and the shrill steam-whistle," Whitman wrote. "I hear the echoes reverberate through the grandest scenery in the world." He viewed these changes as a triumph for democracy, and he applauded them.

In later life Whitman stated, "I know very well that my 'Leaves' could not possibly have emerged or been fashion'd or completed, from any other era than the latter half of the Nineteenth Century, nor any other land than democratic America . . ."

But during the nineteenth century, Americans saw their democratic nation torn apart. In the Civil War, which lasted from 1861 until 1865, the North fought against eleven Southern states that had broken away to form their own nation. This long and bloody war took more than six hundred thousand lives. Another six hundred thousand soldiers were wounded.

Walt Whitman traveled to Washington, D.C., during the Civil

War. There, he cared for countless wounded soldiers in the city's many hospitals. He listened to their tales of battle. He wished them well when they recovered, and grieved when they died. The poems Whitman wrote during the war years—a group called *Drum-Taps*—are some of the finest writing to come out of the Civil War.

Whitman also grieved deeply at the death of Abraham Lincoln, the president who led his nation to victory in the Civil War. Lincoln was "the sweetest, wisest soul of all my days and lands," Whitman believed. He expressed his sorrow in poems that continue to stir people's emotions.

Today, Walt Whitman is considered one of America's greatest poets. But in 1855, when he rode the Fulton Ferry, few people had read his verses. Even fewer recognized their importance. Whitman's poems lacked the careful rhymes and strict rhythms his readers were used to. He wrote joyfully about the human body, and this offended many who wore the high collars and long skirts of the nineteenth century. Critics labeled his work "reckless and indecent," as well as "trashy, profane & obscene."

There were some, however, who understood what Whitman had accomplished. The New England writer Ralph Waldo Emerson called *Leaves of Grass* "the most extraordinary piece of wit & wisdom that America has yet contributed."

As Whitman grew older, he saw his work gain appreciation in Europe and the United States. More and more readers were touched by the deep love of humanity that his poems conveyed. They recognized beauty in his choice of simple words. Today, *Leaves of Grass* is considered a classic work of American literature.

Walt Whitman has been dead for a hundred years. Yet when people read such poems as "Crossing Brooklyn Ferry," they often feel that the author is speaking directly to them. "Closer yet I approach you," Whitman tells them. "Who knows, for all the distance, but I am as good as looking at you now, for all you cannot see me?" He will go on to touch the readers of many generations to come.

"Flood-tide below me! I see you face to face!"

The Whitman home in West Hills, Long Island.

CHAPTER TWO

Flashes and Specks

There was a child went forth every day,
And the first object he look'd upon, that object he became . . .

*W*HEN WALTER WHITMAN, JR., was born, on May 31, 1819, the United States of America was not yet forty-three years old. There were people still alive who had witnessed the American Revolution. "I remember when a boy hearing grandmother Whitman tell about the times of the revolutionary war," Whitman later wrote in his memoirs. Sitting before the hearth in her large farmhouse kitchen, his grandmother told the boy about a battle that took place on Long Island, New York, where the Whitmans lived. "The British had full swing over Long Island, and foraged everywhere, and committed the most horrible excesses," Walt recalled learning from his grandmother.

The battle of August 27, 1776, had been an easy victory for the well-trained British soldiers. With a swift second attack on the American army, England could have won the war. But General George Washington refused to let that happen. On the foggy night of August 28, he silently moved his men off Long Island by boat. The army survived to fight other battles. Under Washington's leadership, the Americans won the war.

The struggle for democracy had created heroes. From his earliest days, Walt heard about George Washington and about Thomas Jefferson, author of the Declaration of Independence, who was still alive in Virginia. He learned of Andrew Jackson, who had won important battles against the British in the War of 1812. Walt's own father had met Thomas Paine, whose pamphlet *Common Sense* had influenced many colonists to fight against English rule.

It was a hopeful, exciting time to be born. The wars with England were over, and the United States was at peace. Settlers were moving west into the lands beyond the Appalachian Mountains. Democratic government was still a new experiment. The boy and his nation could grow up together.

Walt was the second son born to Walter Whitman, Sr., and his wife, Louisa. The Whitmans were a farming family living in West Hills, near the town of Huntington, on Long Island. Flat, sandy Long Island was called Paumanok by the Native Americans who first lived there. Some 120 miles long, the island stretches eastward from New York Bay.

For generations, the Whitmans had lived a life of hard work that bred strong men and women. The men labored in their fields and tended herds of cattle and sheep. The women cooked meals, baked bread, and preserved food for winter. They made clothing and household items, and cared for the children. The family ate vegetables and grain that they grew, and they butchered livestock for meat. Homemade apple cider was their favorite beverage—they drank it with nearly every meal.

Walt was born in a two-story house with wide-planked floors that his father built by hand. "He was a first rate carpenter," Walt said of his father, a man who "did solid, substantial, conscientious work."

Walter Whitman, Sr., was a skilled craftsman, but a glum, pessimistic man. "Keep a good heart," he liked to say, "the worst is to come." Like many Long Island farmers at that time, he drank heavily. As an adult, Walt confided to a friend that his father was "addicted to alcohol." Walter Whitman, Sr., could display a fiery temper when under the influence of liquor.

Walt's father may have been difficult when he was drinking, but he was a bright and thinking person. He read political books and

Walter Whitman, Sr.   *Louisa Whitman, the poet's mother.*

pamphlets. He subscribed to a newspaper, the *Free Enquirer,* that dealt with new, sometimes radical ideas. Walter Whitman, Sr., taught his children to think for themselves. He taught them to value democracy, a system that gave power and dignity to the common people.

The Whitmans were "a stalwart, massive, heavy, long-lived race," Walt reported. The first Whitmans had come to America from England in 1640. There had been Whitmans on Long Island since 1664. Walt had memories of a great-grandmother who smoked tobacco, swore, and handled the most spirited horses. A widow, she had supervised the African-American slaves who worked on her farm.

Slavery was legal in New York until Walt was eight years old. As a young child, Walt saw slaves in his grandmother's kitchen. They would be "squatting on the floor," he wrote, "eating their supper of Indian pudding and milk."

Louisa Whitman's family, the Van Velsors, were descendants of early Dutch settlers. They were prosperous farmers, known for raising fine horses. "My mother, as a young woman, was a daily and daring rider," Walt stated. Louisa Whitman was big, strong, and rosy-faced. She impressed young Walt with her gift for using language. "She could tell stories, impersonate," Walt recalled. "She was very eloquent in the utterance of noble moral axioms—was very original in her manner, her style."

To his mother, Walt seemed different from his older brother, Jesse, and the other farm boys she knew. "He was a very good, but very strange boy," she said. Walt was an imaginative child and an intense observer of the world around him. He experienced a multitude of sensations—sights and sounds, textures and smells—and absorbed them all into his keen memory.

Whitman later wrote a poem that depicts a child interacting closely with his surroundings. The impressions made on his mind were so powerful that the child seemed to become one with the plants and animals he saw. Many readers believe this poem describes the poet's own childhood imaginings. Whitman wrote:

> *There was a child went forth every day,*
> *And the first object he look'd upon, that object he became,*
> *And that object became part of him for the day or a certain*
>   *part of the day,*
> *Or for many years or stretching cycles of years.*

Flowers and birds' songs became part of the child. He was one with the newborn barnyard animals of spring: foals and calves, chicks and ducklings, "the Third-month lambs and the sow's pink-faint litter." He marveled at the stillness of fish suspended in pond water, and the soft, fluid movements of aquatic plants.

Walt went with Jesse and the boys from nearby farms to the Great South Bay, on Long Island's southern shore. "One sport I was very fond of was to go on a bay-party in summer to gather sea-gull's eggs," he remembered. "The gulls lay two or three eggs, more than half the size of hen's eggs, right on the sand, and leave the sun's heat to hatch them."

In winter, the children fished for eels through the frozen surface of the bay. "We would cut holes in the ice, sometimes striking quite an eel-bonanza, and filling our baskets with great, fat, sweet, white-meated fellows," Whitman later wrote. "The scenes, the ice, drawing the hand-sled, cutting holes, spearing the eels, &c., were of course just such fun as is dearest to boyhood."

Whitman made use of these childhood memories when he began to write poetry. "The shores of this bay, winter and summer, and my doings there in early life, are woven all through [*Leaves of Grass*]," he explained.

Young Walt visited the Hempstead plains, in the middle of Long Island. There, he saw a place that was "quite prairie-like, open, uninhabited, rather sterile, covered with kill-calf and huckleberry bushes." Farmers from the surrounding towns brought their cattle to

The town of Huntington, Long Island, depicted in this 1841 woodcut, was proud of its wind-powered sawmill (shown at left).

graze on the plains. The farmers returned in the evenings to walk their cattle home. "I have often been out on the edges of these plains toward sundown," Whitman stated as an adult, "and can yet recall in fancy the interminable cow processions, and hear the music of the tin or copper bells clanking far and near, and breathe the cool of the sweet and slightly aromatic evening air, and note the sunset."

Walt's strong legs carried him up Jayne's Hill, the highest point on Long Island, which was half a mile from the Whitman home. With his black hair blown by the wind, he looked out on the bay and the Atlantic Ocean to the south. Facing north he looked across Long Island Sound to the Connecticut shore.

The beaches were often in Walt's thoughts. He claimed that from his home, he could hear the pounding surf in the stillness following storms. Through his senses, the boy took in images so vivid that he sometimes wondered if they were real. Like the child in his poem, Whitman may have experienced "The doubts of day-time and the doubts of night-time, the curious whether and how." He may have asked himself "Whether that which appears so is so, or is it all flashes and specks?"

In May 1823, Walter Whitman, Sr., decided to give up farming and find a better way to make a living. He moved his family, which now included two daughters, to Brooklyn. Situated on Long Island's western end, Brooklyn was the third largest city in the United States. Brooklyn's population was growing rapidly, and Walt's father hoped to make money building and buying houses, and then selling them at a profit.

The plan sounded good, but it failed. Walter Whitman, Sr., had trouble paying the mortgages on the houses and land he bought. Many times, he lost his property to the banks that had loaned him money. Walt remembered moving into a new house every year. The family lived on Front Street in 1823, on Cranberry Street in 1824, and on Johnson Street in 1825. In 1826, they moved into a house across the street from their old one.

In 1827, the Whitmans lived on Adams Street, and there were five children in the family. Walt attended District School Number One. At that time, teachers demanded strict obedience from their pupils. Children who disobeyed—who failed to memorize a lesson, spoke out of turn, or fidgeted in their seats—received whippings with birch rods or leather straps. The teachers also had "other ingenious methods of child torture," Whitman recalled.

One of Walt's teachers remembered him as a big and clumsy boy, good-natured and sloppily dressed. Walt disliked the school's strictness—he would balk at rules and schedules all of his life. He was an ordinary student, and his later achievements surprised the teacher greatly. His success proved that "We need never be discouraged over anyone," the teacher said.

Life outside of school was much more interesting. Brooklyn presented Walt's impressionable mind with many lively sensations. Again he wondered whether what he saw was real. "Men and women crowding fast in the streets," the child in his poem asked, "if they are not flashes and specks what are they?" City sights—

> *The streets themselves and the façades of houses, and goods in*
> *   the windows,*
> *Vehicles, teams, the heavy-plank'd wharves, the huge crossing*
> *   at the ferries . . .*
> *. . . . .*
> *These became part of that child who went forth every day . . .*

There was always something to see on Fulton Street, a bustling, tree-lined Brooklyn thoroughfare. On July 4, 1825, the marquis de Lafayette traveled along Fulton Street in an open carriage. Lafayette, a French statesman, was a hero of the American Revolution. A great believer in democracy, he had served with George Washington during the war.

Walt was one of a group of schoolchildren who followed Lafayette's carriage down the street. The marquis had come to Brooklyn to lay the cornerstone for a new library. When he stepped down from

Ferries carried people, animals, and wagons between Brooklyn and Manhattan.

his carriage and into the large hole that had been dug for the library's cellar, the children crowded around to watch.

Lafayette had noticed his young audience. One by one, he picked up the children and lowered them into the cellar, so they could view the ceremony up close. Walt felt "childish pride," he said, to be "one of those who were taken in the arms of Lafayette and reached down by him to a standing place."

In June 1829, the children followed another procession on Fulton Street. The occasion was a spectacular funeral march. More than forty crewmen had died when a steamship exploded in the Brooklyn Navy Yard. Walt recalled "the sailors marching two by two, hand in hand, banners tied up and bound in black crepe, the muffled drums beating, the bugles wailing for the mournful peals of a dead march."

Whitman remembered it all, he said. He remembered "the soldiers firing the salute over the grave. And then how everything changed with the dashing and merry jig played by the same bugles and drums, as they made exit from the graveyard and wended rapidly home."

The painful discipline of school and the freedom to roam Brooklyn's streets filled only a few short years in Whitman's life. When he was eleven years old, his parents decided it was time for him to leave school. The impressionable child had absorbed the sensations of the farmyard, seashore, and city streets. Now it was time for him to go forth into the working world.

Workers in nineteenth-century printshops set type and operated presses by hand.

CHAPTER THREE

A First-Rate Loafer

*I possessed almost unlimited capacity
for floating on my back.*

❧❦❧

WALT BEGAN his working life as an office boy at a Fulton Street law firm. It was the first of many jobs he would hold over the next twenty-five years, as he helped support the large Whitman family. He never returned to the formal studies of school, but he never stopped learning.

Walt's first employers, lawyer James B. Clarke and his son Edward, took an interest in their young clerk's education. "Edward C. kindly help'd me at my handwriting and composition," Whitman noted. The lawyers also obtained a library card for Walt and urged him to read in his spare time. The sensitive boy felt swept away by the fabulous stories he discovered in novels and poems. "I now revel'd in romance-reading of all kinds," Whitman explained. "First, the 'Arabian Nights,' all the volumes, an amazing treat."

In the writings of the Scottish novelist Sir Walter Scott, Walt read tales drawn from old ballads and legends. He followed the exploits of medieval knights and eighteenth-century heroes. Walt also enjoyed the action-packed novels of an American author, James Fenimore Cooper. Cooper glorified American life in the wilderness and at sea. Walt read *The Spy*, an exciting tale of the Revolutionary War. In another Cooper novel, *The Last of the Mohicans*, Walt thrilled at the adventures of frontiersman Natty Bumppo.

James and Edward Clarke sometimes sent Walt on errands, giving him a chance to explore the Brooklyn waterfront. Walt delivered legal papers to the shipyards, where craftsmen turned boards and timber into the hulls and masts of sailing ships. He carried messages to the distilleries, where whiskey was produced.

At times, the Clarkes asked Walt to run errands in Manhattan. This meant riding the ferry, and possibly coming face-to-face with famous Americans. On one winter trip to Manhattan, Walt spotted the wealthiest man in the country, John Jacob Astor. The sight of the stout, feeble old man, "bearded, swathed in rich furs, with a great ermine cap on his head," remained in Whitman's memory. A throng of servants helped Astor down the steps of his home and then tucked him into a luxurious sleigh. "The sleigh was drawn by as fine a team of horses as I ever saw," Whitman remembered.

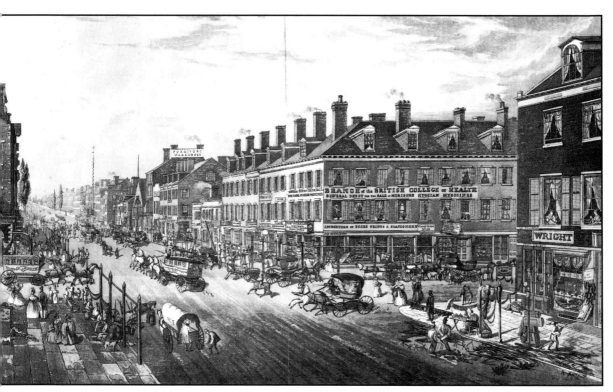

Broadway in the 1830s—a lively, noisy thoroughfare.

More than once, Walt brought documents to Aaron Burr. The aging former vice-president of the United States, notorious for killing Alexander Hamilton in a duel, was ending his career quietly, by working as an attorney. Whitman never forgot Burr's demeanor, his "alertness, smiling old eyes, and hearty laugh." Burr took a grandfatherly pleasure in his young visitor. "He had a way of giving me a bit of fruit on these occasions—an apple or a pear," Whitman said.

William Hartshorne was another old man who took a liking to Walt. They met when Walt was twelve and had a new job, as an apprentice at a newspaper, the *Long Island Patriot*. Hartshorne had grown up in Philadelphia during the American Revolution. In the basement composing room where he taught Walt to set type for printing, he reminisced about the great men he had met—George Washington, Thomas Jefferson, and Benjamin Franklin.

With his old-fashioned ways, Hartshorne himself seemed to be a relic from the past. "He had the old-school manner," wrote Whitman, "rather sedate, not fast, never too familiar, always restraining his temper, always cheerful, benevolent, friendly, observing all the decorums of language and action."

By the summer of 1832, Walt had left William Hartshorne and the *Patriot* to work for another Brooklyn newspaper, the *Star*. At that time, the number of newspapers in the United States was growing rapidly. There were thirty-six dailies in 1830. By 1850, there would be 254. The residents of populous communities such as Brooklyn or New York City could take their pick from several competing papers.

The Whitman family was growing, too. In 1833, Louisa gave birth to the boy who would always be Walt's favorite brother, Thomas Jefferson Whitman, whom the family called Jeff. Soon after Jeff's birth, Walter Whitman, Sr., gave up the building trade and moved his family back to their Long Island farm. Walt, however, remained in Brooklyn to continue earning a paycheck. He finished his apprenticeship and started work as a journeyman, or beginning, printer.

At sixteen, Walt was nearly full grown, looking more like a man than a boy. He "grew too fast," he said about himself. Walt still liked

A poster advertising one of the popular melodramas shown at a New York theater.

to read, but he had found a new love—the theater. He went to see many of the melodramas that were popular in the nineteenth century, plays with such sensational titles as *The Last Days of Pompeii* and *The Murder at the Roadside Inn*. The melodramas pitted a virtuous hero against a wicked villain. The hero often had to fight battles or survive volcanic eruptions, earthquakes, or other disasters before good could triumph over evil.

Whitman also saw several plays by William Shakespeare. He was so moved by seeing the renowned actor Edwin Booth starring in Shakespeare's *Richard III* that many years later, he could relive every detail of Booth's entrance into the theater on that night. "With head bent, he slowly and in silence (amid the tempest of boistrous hand-clapping) walks down the stage to the foot-lights with that peculiar

The well-known actor Edwin Booth.

abstracted gesture, musingly kicking his sword, which he holds off from him by its sash," Whitman related. "Though fifty years have passed since then, I can hear the clank and feel the perfect following hush of perhaps 3,000 people waiting."

At first, Walt went to the theater with other young men from the printshops. But he soon preferred to attend alone. "I was so absorbed in the performance, and disliked anyone to distract my attention," he said.

It was at this time in his life, while still a teenager, that Walt felt the initial urge to write. He felt inspired, he said, when visiting the New York waterfront, "when I saw a ship under full sail, and had the desire to describe it exactly as it seemed to me." He wrote short articles for the *Mirror*, a New York newspaper. Those articles were printed without a byline, however, and scholars have been unable to distinguish Whitman's work from the many stories by other writers that appeared on the pages of the *Mirror*.

In December 1835, disaster interrupted Whitman's writing career. He was working as a typesetter in Manhattan when a series of fires destroyed a large commercial section of the city. Flames leveled warehouses and elegant shops. They demolished Paternoster Row, the center of New York's newspaper publishing industry.

New Yorkers saw costly silks and laces, singed by fire and ruined by water, pulled from the burned-out shops. Whole cargoes of coffee and tea, damaged and worthless, were dumped onto the muddy streets. With printing presses, newsprint, and their places of business destroyed, many newspaper workers—including Walt Whitman—lost their jobs. Walt returned to Long Island to live with his family.

Those first months back in West Hills were a difficult time for Whitman. He was fast becoming a young man, yet was confused about the direction his life should take. He had made up his mind about one thing, though. He did not want to be a farmer. Walt and his father argued fiercely that summer over his refusal to feed livestock or push a plow.

It was much more pleasant to spend the day at the ocean. "I was

Flames lit up the sky and caused vast damage in Manhattan in 1835.

a first rate aquatic loafer," Whitman boasted. "I possessed almost unlimited capacity for floating on my back."

Spending time with his brothers and sisters also gave Walt pleasure. "There was a growing family of children—eight of us—my brother Jesse the oldest, myself the second, my dear sisters Mary and Hannah Louisa, my brothers Andrew, George, Thomas Jefferson, and then my youngest brother, Edward, born 1835, and always badly crippled," Whitman stated. The poet's brother Edward, called Eddy by the family, was disabled mentally as well as physically. He appears to have been afflicted with mental retardation and epilepsy.

Seventeen-year-old Walt found employment when autumn arrived. Although he had little formal training himself, he became a teacher, instructing the local farmers' sons in reading, writing, arithmetic, grammar, and geography.

The country school was nothing more than a shack, and the pay was poor. Walt boarded with the families of his pupils, moving from farm to farm. One family asked him to spend the night in their barn, sleeping beside a sick cow! He often felt lonely in the evenings and

Pupils posed with their teacher in 1893, outside the Old Woodbury School, where Walt Whitman once taught.

passed the time playing checkers by himself. Still, Whitman continued to observe his surroundings keenly. He considered boarding with the farm families to be "one of my best experiences and deepest lessons in human nature behind the scenes, and in the masses."

What kind of teacher did Walt Whitman prove to be? His brother George, who was one of his pupils, remembered that "Walt made a very good schoolmaster." Walt's refusal to give whippings made him popular with the schoolboys. He liked to join them in games of baseball and cards. His employers, however, found fault with Whitman's teaching style. The young educator often sat at his desk writing and daydreaming when he should have been instructing, members of the school board complained. When his contract expired, it was not renewed.

Walt turned to the one enterprise in which he had experience—newspapers. With business partners who provided financial backing, he bought a printing press and rented office space above a stable. In June 1838, he began printing his own newspaper, the *Long Islander*. This weekly paper carried stories of interest to the local people, such as harvest and weather reports. Occasionally, Whitman had a big news story to write, as when lightning took the life of a Long Island farmer.

Riding his white horse, Nina, Whitman delivered each new issue of the *Long Islander* to the farmers of Huntington and the nearby towns: Commack, Smithtown, and Babylon. Often a farming family, hungry for company, invited him to share a meal or spend the night. Whitman accepted their invitations with pleasure. He later looked back with fondness on his travels with Nina and these simple visits. "I never had happier jaunts," he said.

When his business partners sold the *Long Islander* in the summer of 1839, Walt Whitman was out of a job once more. He sold Nina and moved to Manhattan, where he drifted from one position to another. He worked in the newspaper field and even tried teaching again. Walt's employers liked his easygoing nature, but his work habits drove them crazy. His editor at the *Democrat* believed that Walt showed promise as a reporter. Why, then, the editor wanted to know, could he not work regular hours? If Walt left the office for lunch, he was likely to lose track of the time. The editor might find him outside hours later, gazing into the sky.

Walt valued his ability to relax, believing it set him apart from the normal run of hardworking nineteenth-century men and women. "Of all human beings, none equals your genuine, inborn, unvarying loafer," he believed. "What was Adam, I should like to know, but a loafer?"

Most people saw Walt Whitman as a calm, slow-moving man. He was his father's son, though, and on rare occasions, without warning, his temper flared. One of his angry outbursts occurred during an Episcopal service. The Episcopal Church asks men to remove their hats for worship, but Walt had left his on. When an usher removed the hat for him, Walt saw red. He grabbed the hat, twisted it up, and used it to beat the usher's head. Then he stormed furiously out of the church.

In 1841, Walt moved into a Manhattan Island boardinghouse. Immigration and the city's growing reputation as a commercial center had caused its population to soar. The population had grown from fewer than seventy thousand in 1800 to three hundred thousand in 1837. At that rate, people speculated, it could reach two million by the turn of the century!

Housing was expensive and hard to find, so many bachelors and newlyweds lived in the city's boardinghouses. They ate their meals at refectories, plain, cheap restaurants that stayed open all hours of the day and night. Because Manhattan's thirty hotels could take in only a fraction of the city's visitors, tourists frequented the boarding-houses, too.

Walt began to take an interest in his appearance at this time. He became one of the fashionable young men who dressed up in English-style suits and called themselves dandies. With a flower in his lapel, a polished cane grasped firmly in his hand, and a high hat balanced on his thick hair, he walked the city streets. The numbered

Walt Whitman in his twenties, dressed as a dandy.

avenues and streets conformed to a grid pattern laid out in 1811. The long artery called Broadway cut across Manhattan diagonally, and was noisy with the clatter of horse-drawn vehicles. Walt roamed from the north of the island, where houses were being built on farmland, to the south, where Irish and German immigrants lived in crowded neighborhoods.

Whitman recalled "Looking in at the shop-windows of Broadway the whole forenoon, flatting the flesh of my nose on the thick plate glass . . ." He watched policemen walking their beat and women posing for portrait photographers. At these times, he tried to empty his mind of thoughts and to soak up the impressions that surrounded him.

Whitman watched the movements of laborers so closely that he later would be able to describe them vividly. As a group of black-smiths raised their heavy sledges, Whitman noted in one of his poems:

> The lithe sheer of their waists plays even with their
>   massive arms,
> Overhand the hammers swing, overhand so slow, overhand
>   so sure,
> They do not hasten, each man hits in his place.

Whitman now spent his working hours in the pressroom of the *New World*, a periodical that devoted most of its pages to the work of British writers. Because no copyright agreements existed between England and the United States at that time, American publishers could reprint the work of any English author at no cost. The editors of the *New World* devoted many of their large pages to the latest novels of Charles Dickens, which they printed a chapter or two at a time.

The *New World* did include some stories and articles written by Americans, even some by Walt Whitman. But educated readers preferred literature from England, the nation of refinement, culture,

In cities and towns across America, blacksmiths hammered hot iron to make shoes for horses.

and scholarship. England was the land of Shakespeare. It had given the world such great poets as Percy Bysshe Shelley and John Keats, who chose Greek and Roman gods as their subjects, and Alfred Tennyson, who had drawn upon the legends of King Arthur.

America, in contrast, was perceived by people on both sides of the Atlantic to be a rough land, only partly civilized. American culture was based on tall tales, woodlands, and log cabins. America would never produce great literature, some critics claimed, because Europe was the source of all great ideas. What could America contribute besides Paul Bunyan and Natty Bumppo?

One American writer seemed to be an exception to the rule. Ralph Waldo Emerson of Massachusetts had expressed some original ideas in his essays and poems, ideas that even people in England took

Ralph Waldo Emerson.

seriously. A man who had broken with organized religion, Emerson believed in the existence of a supreme intelligence, or universal mind, which he called the Over-Soul. He taught that every person's consciousness was part of the Over-Soul. "Within man is the soul of the whole," he wrote. By building a relationship with the Over-Soul, Emerson preached, individuals could transcend, or move beyond ordinary experience. The Over-Soul would lead them into new levels of understanding. Followers of this philosophy, known as transcendentalism, saw evidence of the Over-Soul in nature. They valued time spent in natural settings.

In March 1842, Emerson gave a lecture in New York City, and Walt Whitman was in the audience. Emerson spoke that night about the future of poetry in America. He voiced his belief that the vast American continent would one day spawn a great poet.

"The genius of poetry is here," Emerson said. "He is in the forest walks, in paths carpeted with leaves of the chestnut, oak, and pine; he sits on the mosses of the mountain, he listens by the echoes of the wood; he paddles his canoe in the rivers and ponds." To doubt that America, with its limitless natural beauty, would produce a great poet would be "to doubt of day and night," Emerson concluded.

Walt listened enthusiastically as Emerson stated ideas that complemented his own. Like Emerson, he saw potential in the raw, unfinished United States. "We forget that God has given the American mind powers of analysis and acuteness superior to those possessed by any other nation on earth," Whitman said.

Emerson had inspired Whitman to work at his own writing, but the results were disappointing. Walt wrote several stories for magazines, melodramatic tales of cruel fathers and misunderstood young men. He even published a novel, *Franklin Evans*. It told the sad, sentimental story of a young man from a Long Island farm who met up with bad friends and began drinking heavily. Whitman felt little pride in this book, and quickly decided he would write no more like it. "It was damned rot—rot of the worst sort," he said of *Franklin Evans*. "It was not the business for me to be up to. I stopped right there; I never cut a chip off that kind of timber again."

But would he ever find the right kind of business to be up to? By September 1845, when he moved back to Brooklyn, he had been employed by ten newspapers and had yet to put his heart into his work. "There is a man about our office so lazy that it takes two men to open his jaws when he speaks," complained one of his exasperated bosses. "If you kick him he's too idle to cry, for then he'd have to wipe his eyes. *What* can be done with him?"

Whitman did manage to hold a job with one newspaper for two years. Working conditions at Brooklyn's largest newspaper, the *Daily Eagle*, suited him to a T. The paper offered "a good owner, good pay, and easy work and hours," Walt remarked. He used some of his ample salary to help his family buy a house in Brooklyn, as well as some furnishings, when Walter Whitman, Sr., gave up farming. He treated his family to gifts—boots for his brothers and jewelry and sewing supplies for his mother and sisters.

While working for the *Daily Eagle*, Whitman marveled at how the telegraph, a new invention, enabled news to travel "in the twinkling of an eye" from one location to another. "The governor's message, which we publish today, was transmitted, (5,000 words) from Albany to New York yesterday," he noted on one occasion. The message arrived at the *Eagle* offices after noon, but it was "in type, printed, and for sale in Brooklyn and New York by 4 o'clock!"

Whitman wrote a number of editorials, or opinion pieces, that appeared on the pages of the *Eagle*. One of his editorials called for brighter streetlights. Another protested against showy architecture in churches.

Still another of Whitman's editorials urged the people of Brooklyn to bathe more often. "Brooklyn would be a healthier city even than it is," he wrote, "if the semi-weekly bath, during the summer, were a rigid rule for *all* our citizens—for all ages and both sexes." As someone who bathed daily, Whitman believed bathing improved the complexion and brought out people's beauty.

The good pay and steady employment ended in early 1848, when the publishers of the *Daily Eagle* fired Walt Whitman. The reason for his termination is unclear. According to Walt, he left due to political differences with his bosses. Yet a rumor circulated in the publishing world that Whitman's temper had exploded again, and that he had kicked a visiting politician down the office stairs.

Whitman's employers dismissed the rumor, though. "Whoever knows him will laugh at the idea of his *kicking any body*, much less a prominent politician," one of them wrote. "He is too indolent to kick a musketo."

Steamboats carried passengers and cargo between ports on the Mississippi River.

CHAPTER FOUR

Simmering

*Lumber the writing with nothing—let it go as lightly as a
bird flies in the air—or a fish swims in the sea.*

$\mathcal{J}$OBLESSNESS DID NOT keep Walt Whitman from enjoying Manhattan's entertainments. On February 9, 1848, he attended a play at the Broadway Theatre and ran into another newspaperman, J. E. McClure. McClure was starting a daily paper in New Orleans, to be called the *Crescent*. He offered Walt a job. The fired *Eagle* editor accepted the offer quickly, on impulse. Two days later, with his belongings packed in a trunk, he began his journey south. Walt's fourteen-year-old brother, Jeff, accompanied him.

They traveled by train and coach to Wheeling, Virginia (now part of West Virginia), where they boarded a steamboat. The trip down the Ohio and Mississippi rivers to Louisiana took twelve days. Walt and Jeff slept comfortably in their plush stateroom and filled their plates with the rich food served to the passengers. Roasted meats, steaks, sausages, pies, puddings—the luxury aboard ship equaled anything patrons might enjoy at the Astor House, an elegant New York hotel, the brothers agreed.

Just once, the ride turned treacherous. Navigating past the Kentucky shore, the pilot chose to bypass a calm canal and to steer the boat over some rough water. "The *fright* we all had," Jeff wrote to his mother. "If the boat had sunk we were within a few feet of the shore, but I don't think we could have got there, the current was so swift."

35

The steamboat entered crowded waters as it approached the busy port of New Orleans, with its many office buildings and warehouses. Walt and Jeff sailed past ferries, fishing boats, and even oceangoing vessels. They saw dock workers loading ships with cargoes of grain and cotton, and unloading crates of coffee and cocoa. The workers called to each other in an exotic mixture of French and English.

The Whitmans settled in rooms across the street from the *Crescent* offices. Jeff worked as an office boy for the paper, while Walt was its exchange editor. He "made up the news," he said, with a "pen and scissors." Each day, he read the many newspapers that arrived by mail from other cities. He cut out the most interesting articles and then rewrote them for the *Crescent*.

Jeff Whitman as an adult.

Hungry for sights and sensations as always, Whitman used his free time to explore New Orleans. He found streets that were alive with colors and aromas. Peddlers hawked fresh-caught crabs, and young women sold flowers in the morning sun. "The persons employed in fancy stores were bedecking their windows with the gaudiest goods, and the savory smell of fried ham, broiled beef-steaks, with onions, etc., stole forth from the half unshut doors of every restaurant," Whitman noted.

His walks took him through parks where idle soldiers camped and loitered. These men had fought in the Mexican War, which arose from America's hunger for land. On May 12, 1846, the United States had declared war on Mexico, following a border dispute. The war ended with a treaty signed on February 2, 1848, which established the Texas-Mexico border at the Rio Grande. The treaty gave the United States the future states of California and New Mexico.

Whitman, the champion of democracy, had cheered the victory. Like many Americans, he embraced the concept of Manifest Destiny. According to this political doctrine, the United States was destined to grow westward to the Pacific Ocean. Some people even claimed that this was God's plan. Whitman had spoken out in support of the war in the pages of the *Eagle*. "Cold must be the pulse, and throbless to all good thoughts—no true American's will it be—which cannot respond to the valorous emprise of our soldiers and commanders in Mexico," he wrote.

One aspect of the victory in Mexico troubled him. He feared that Southern slavery might spread into the new land. The South had built an economy based on slave labor. Nearly four million African-American slaves worked long hours in the fields and plantation homes of the South to provide profit and comfort for their owners.

Whitman opposed the spread of slavery, which ran contrary to the democratic ideal of personal freedom. "If there are any States to be formed out of the territory lately annexed," he asserted, "*Slavery must be prohibited in them forever.*"

New Orleans brought Walt Whitman face-to-face with the slave

Slave auctions were common sights in the South before the Civil War.

trade of the South. He saw public slave auctions and read ads from slave traders that were printed in the *Crescent*. He was repelled by the buying and selling of human beings. Later, in his poetry, he would express his outrage over "A man's body at auction":

> *Gentlemen look on this wonder,*
> *Whatever the bids of the bidders they cannot be high enough for it . . .*
> *. . . . .*
> *In this head the all-baffling brain,*
> *In it and below it the makings of heroes . . .*
> *. . . . .*
> *Within there runs blood,*
> *The same old blood! the same red-running blood!*
> *There swells and jets a heart, there all passions, desires,*
>   *reachings, aspirations . . .*

At first Walt had found New Orleans to be "a great place and *no* mistake," but slavery soon cast a shadow over his enjoyment of the city. And within months, he and Jeff grew deeply homesick. Few letters arrived from New York, and Walt worried about his family. "If you only keep well till I get home again," he wrote to his mother, "I think I shall be satisfied."

By this time, McClure had grown fed up with his new editor. He and Whitman disagreed openly about slavery. They argued over money. After a quarrel in late May, Walt and Jeff packed their bags and returned to New York.

Excited over the slavery issue, Walt Whitman joined the new Free-Soil party. This political organization opposed the spread of slavery into new states and territories. Whitman went as a delegate to the party's national convention in Buffalo, New York. In September 1848, he started a Free-Soil newspaper, the *Brooklyn Freeman*, and kept it going for a year.

The real estate business was booming in Brooklyn in 1849. Tired now of politics, Walt went into the building trade with his father and brothers. He called himself a carpenter, but he handled the paperwork and accounting for the business while the others sawed and hammered. His brother George observed that Walt "made a living now—wrote a little, worked a little, loafed a little." Walt wrote articles for the New York newspapers from time to time.

The Whitmans operated their carpentry business from this Brooklyn site.

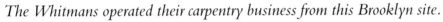

Whitman dated this photograph of himself 1849. Some scholars think 1856 is more likely the correct date.

Walt Whitman
1849

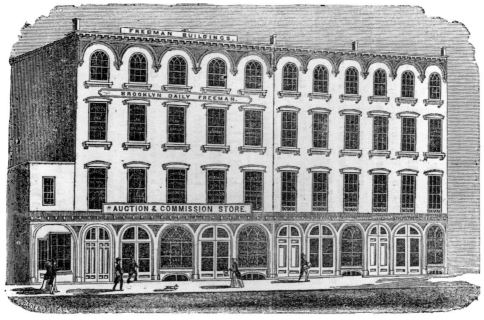

The offices of the Brooklyn Daily Freeman *on Fulton Street.*

The Whitmans lived together in one house, and the family learned to put up with Walt's odd habits. As George Whitman observed, "If we had dinner at one, like as not he would come at three: always late. Just as we were fixing things on the table, he would get up and go around the block."

Another comment of George's showed that Walt retained the finely tuned senses of his childhood. "Walt's hearing was very acute, especially at night," George said. "Noises in the street he would growl about. He seemed to hear sounds others did not hear or take notice of. His sense of smell, too, was remarkable."

Walt supervised the building of a new family house on Myrtle Avenue, one with space for a bookstore and printshop on the first floor. Walt was to run these businesses, but he must have had few customers. He had time to range all over Brooklyn and Manhattan, seeking people and places that stimulated his mind. He entered a period of great personal growth. These were "days of preparation: the gathering of the forces," Whitman noted.

He still wanted to be a writer, but thought he lacked the necessary education. Whitman set about educating himself. He read articles on a wide variety of subjects, from Darwin's recent theory of evolution to the structure of the earth. He delved into religion and history.

Whitman was "simmering," he said. His newfound knowledge bubbled gently in his mind, like the ingredients of a savory stew. And just as a chef combines meat, vegetables, and spices to create a real stew, Whitman would one day blend the varied facts and ideas in his mind to create his poetry.

One subject that interested Walt greatly was phrenology. Phrenologists tried to explain human psychology by studying the bumps on the head. The bumps were related to the structure of the brain, they said. They drew elaborate charts of the brain showing the sections that controlled various personal traits, such as self-esteem, hope, and mirth. Some of the qualities they identified had strange names—alimentiveness, for example, or philoprogenitiveness—and obscure meanings.

Phrenologists never actually painted on people's scalps, as shown in this cartoon. But they did assert that bumps on the head corresponded to features of the brain.

A bump on the skull over a certain area of the brain meant that the corresponding trait was part of the personality, the phrenologists stated. They insisted their work was scientific, but in truth it had no basis in science. Many nineteenth-century men and women considered it fun to have a phrenologist feel the bumps on their head and draw up a profile of their personality.

"One of the choice places of New York to me then was the 'Phrenological Cabinet' of Fowler and Wells," Whitman later wrote. "Here were all the busts, examples, curios and books of that study obtainable. I went there often, and once for myself had a very elaborate and leisurely examination and 'chart of bumps,' written out."

Whitman also liked to visit Dr. Henry Abbott's private museum.

In his Broadway rooms, Abbott displayed artifacts from ancient Egypt. Walt was "a solitary gazer amid these wonderful relics," he said. He examined mummies, statues of pharaohs and ancient gods, and fragments of papyrus scrolls covered in mysterious hieroglyphics.

He was particularly taken with the myth of Osiris. The early Egyptians regarded the god Osiris as the source of renewed life. According to the myth, Osiris was murdered by his evil brother, who then tore his body to pieces. Buried in the earth, the body sprouted stalks and leaves. Abbott showed Walt ancient drawings of plant life growing from Osiris' corpse.

Some evenings, Whitman went to hear Italian opera, which had just become popular in the United States. "Ah this indeed is music—this suits me," he said. The operas Walt heard had a different structure from music written for the orchestra alone. In the melodic arias, or songs, of opera, characters expressed their innermost feelings. Other passages of opera, known as recitatives, were sung in a rhythm that mimicked everyday speech.

In spite of his trips to the opera house, Whitman had begun to think of himself less as a dandy and more as a "rough," or common man. He put away his stylish suits and wore the flannel shirts and baggy pants of a laborer. He was re-creating himself, and he wanted his appearance to reflect his inner changes.

At age thirty, Whitman described himself as a "tall, large, rough-looking man, in a journeyman carpenter's uniform." He had a "coarse, sanguine complexion," he said, and a "strong, bristly grizzled beard; singular eyes, of a semitransparent, indistinct light blue, and with that sleepy look that comes when the lid rests half way down over the pupil." Finally, he remarked that he had a "careless, lounging gait."

He sought the companionship of working men. He chatted with the pilots on the Fulton Ferry, and rode alongside the Broadway stagecoach drivers. "They had immense qualities, largely animal—eating, drinking, women—great personal pride, in their way—perhaps a few slouches here and there, but I should have trusted the general run of them, in their simple good-will and honor, under all circumstances," Walt wrote of the drivers. Once, when a driver became ill, Walt completed his route for him, and then gave his earnings to the man's family.

During the hot summer of 1853, Walt liked to go with his working-class friends to the World's Fair, inside Manhattan's Crystal Palace. The Crystal Palace was a wonder of nineteenth-century architecture. An iron framework holding fifteen thousand panels of glass, it was a huge octagon covering nearly five acres. At its top was the largest dome in the Western Hemisphere, measuring 123 feet in height and 100 feet in diameter.

America's first World's Fair celebrated technology and progress. All kinds of machinery, from steam and electrical engines to printing

A crowd gathers at the Crystal Palace.

The interior of the Crystal Palace, with a statue of George Washington as its centerpiece.

presses and apple parers, were arranged around the fair's focal point, an enormous statue of George Washington on horseback. There seemed to be nothing American technology could not accomplish.

The arts held promise as well. Whitman made friends with painters, sculptors, and photographers. As he watched them work, he formed ideas about the purpose of art. "To the artist has been given the command to go forth into all the world and preach the gospel of beauty," he said.

Walt carried a small green notebook in his pocket to jot down ideas about his own "gospel of beauty." He was formulating a new way to write poetry—American poetry—that would break with long-held traditions.

"Make it plain," he wrote. "Lumber the writing with nothing— let it go as lightly as a bird flies in the air—or a fish swims in the sea." His goal was "a perfectly transparent, plate-glassy style, artless, with no ornaments." He wanted to write uncluttered poems, poems without fancy words or flourishes that might get in between the writer and the reader.

Whitman's poems would differ greatly from the works of European poets that dealt with myths and stories of kings. "Take no illustrations whatsoever from the ancients or classics," he told himself, "nor from the royal and aristocratic institutions and forms of Europe. Make no mention or allusion to them whatever, except as they relate to the new, present things—to our country—to American character or interests."

When he had filled one notebook, Whitman started another. He sometimes described his city walks. "I often wander all day on Manhattan Island, through streets toward the East River," he wrote one day, "on purpose to have the pleasure of hearing the voices of the native-born and bred workmen and apprentices in the spar-yards, on piers, caulkers on the ship-scaffolds, workmen in iron, mechanics to or from their shops, drivers calling to their horses, and the like."

Writing in his notebooks took up more and more of his time. Used to odd behavior from Walt, his family watched what he did, but asked no questions. "He would lie abed late, and after getting up would write a few hours if he took the notion," George Whitman observed. "We did not know what he was writing."

Walt, however, knew exactly what he was doing. He had finally begun "elaborating the plan of my poems," he said. A lifetime's observations, the rapid learning of recent years, and his ideas about writing poetry had simmered long enough. He was ready to serve up his finished poems. It was a period of "experimenting much," Whitman said, "and writing and abandoning much."

The engraved portrait of Walt Whitman that appeared in the first edition of Leaves of Grass.

CHAPTER FIVE

So Many Uttering Tongues

This hour I tell things in confidence,
I might not tell everybody, but I will tell you.

❧❧❧

THE PRINTSHOP BELONGING to James and Thomas Rome sat at the corner of Fulton and Cranberry streets. During the spring of 1855, Walt Whitman spent most of his days inside the small brick building. He was writing out new verses and revising others, ridding them of "stock touches"—quotations, fancy figures of speech, and references to legends and myths. He was setting the poems in type and correcting mistakes on printed pages.

Whitman was turning his poems into a book. He felt at home around the ink and presses after so many years in the newspaper trade, and he did much of the printing himself.

By early summer, he held the finished book in his hands. It was a slim volume containing twelve untitled poems. The book's green cloth cover bore its title, *Leaves of Grass*, surrounded by leafy tendrils. No author's name appeared on the title page. There was, instead, a portrait of the bearded poet with his plain shirt open at the collar and his hat worn at an angle. The picture showed a man who was vigorous, in glowing health, and very much involved in life.

A careful reader, though, could find the author's name tucked into the long, densely packed lines of poetry:

Walt Whitman, a kosmos, of Manhattan the son,
Turbulent, fleshy, sensual, eating, drinking and breeding . . .

This poet was a complex man who encompassed a cosmos, or universe. He had strong emotions and lusty appetites.

Those lines were part of the book's longest poem, a sprawling, exuberant masterpiece later titled "Song of Myself." Whitman had written in one of his notebooks that he wanted to create "a poem in which all things and qualities and processes express themselves." This was that poem.

In "Song of Myself," the poet portrayed himself as the embodiment of a great life force, someone connected to all of humanity and to God. "And I know that the spirit of God is the brother of my own," Whitman wrote, "And that all the men ever born are also my brothers, and the women my sisters and lovers . . ."

All living things are connected, the poet said. The great force of life links people with tortoises and jays, bay mares and ganders, "The sharp-hoof'd moose of the north, the cat on the house-sill, the chickadee, the prairie dog," and "The litter of the grunting sow as they tug at her teats . . ." People are even linked, Whitman wrote, to the grass growing from the ground.

The long poem explained the meaning of the book's title, *Leaves of Grass*. Echoing the story of Osiris, the Egyptian god whose body sprouted shoots from the soil, Whitman called grass "the beautiful uncut hair of graves." He imagined it growing from the buried dead, "from the breasts of young men" and "from old people, or from offspring taken soon out of their mothers' laps." The grass proves that death is not an end to life, Whitman asserted, but a change in its form. Life follows a cycle of birth, death, and renewal. "All goes onward and outward, nothing collapses."

The pages of Whitman's book were the leaves of grass that sprang

The wild gander leads his flock through the cool night,
Ya-honk! he says, and sounds it down to me like
        an invitation; and meaningless, but I listen closer,
The pert suppose it is meaningless, but I listen closer,
I find its place and sign up there toward
    metaphysed the November sky,—
The moose of the north, the cat on the housesill, the chickadee,
The litter of the grunting sow as they tug at her teats,
The brood of the turkey-hen, and she with her
        half-spread wings,
I see in them and myself the same old law.

The press of my foot to the earth springs a hundred
        affections,
They scorn the best I can do to relate them—

I am enamoured of growing outdoors,
Of men that live among cattle or taste of the
    ocean or soil,
I can eat and sleep with them week in and week out.

What is commonest and cheapest and nearest and easiest is Me,
Me going in for my chances, spending
Spending for vast returns,
Adorning myself to bestow myself on the first
        that will take me,
Not asking the sky to come down to my
        good will,
Scattering it freely forever.—

The pure contralto sings in the organ-loft,
The carpenter dresses his plank,... the tongue of his fore-plane
        whistles its wild ascending lisp,
The married and unmarried children ride home to their
        thanksgiving dinner,
The pilot seizes the king-pin, he heaves down with a strong arm,

Only one page of Whitman's original manuscript of Leaves of Grass
is known to exist.

from his own mind. He would live on after death through his verses. Like "so many uttering tongues," they would speak to the living.

The magnificent self—the "I" of Whitman's poem—shared the experiences of countless other people, including farm boys, Yankee girls, fishermen, and trappers. Whitman imagined himself moving across America and entering simple dramas of daily life. He wrote:

> *The boatmen and clam-diggers arose early and stopt for me,*
> *I tuck'd my trowser-ends in my boots and went and had a good*
>   *time . . .*
> . . . . .
> *The butcher-boy puts off his killing-clothes, or sharpens his*
>   *knife at the stall in the market,*
> *I loiter enjoying his repartee and his shuffle and break-down.*

The life force was so powerful that the poet could even seem to be other people and to feel their pain:

> *I am the hounded slave, I wince at the bite of the dogs . . .*
> . . . .
> *I do not ask the wounded person how he feels, I myself become*
>   *the wounded person.*

The lengthy poem offered a sweeping view of nineteenth-century American life. Newly arrived immigrants inhabited its lines, along with a policeman walking his beat, ballroom dancers, machinists, and a boy listening to the music of rain on his attic roof.

Whitman expressed his love of the earth:

> *Earth of the slumbering and liquid trees!*
> *Earth of departed sunset—earth of the mountains misty-top't! . . .*
> . . . .
> *Far-swooping elbow'd earth—rich apple-blossom'd earth!*

He spoke to the sea, asking it to:

Cushion me soft, rock me in billowy drowse,
. . . .
Sea of stretch'd ground-swells,
Sea breathing broad and convulsive breaths . . .

The poem incorporated Whitman's learning of recent years as it celebrated science and progress:

Hurrah for positive science! long live exact demonstration! . . .
. . . .
This is the lexicographer, this the chemist, this made a grammar
    of the old cartouches,
These mariners put the ship through dangerous unknown seas,
This is the geologist, this works with the scalpel, and this is a
    mathematician.

Larger than life, Whitman seemed to be singing from a mountaintop or from a hot-air balloon traveling east to west, as he scanned North America. At the same time, he claimed to be speaking directly to the reader, whispering thoughts to him or her alone. "This hour I tell things in confidence," he wrote. "I might not tell everybody, but I will tell you."

"Song of Myself" and the other poems in *Leaves of Grass* celebrated the beauty of the human body, inside and out. In a poem later called "I Sing the Body Electric," Whitman praised:

The lung-sponges, the stomach-sac, the bowels sweet and clean,
The brain in its folds inside the skull-frame,
Sympathies, heart-valves, palate-valves, sexuality, maternity . . .
. . . .
The womb, the teats, nipples, breast-milk, tears, laughter, weeping . . .

Nothing about the body was shameful. In "Song of Myself," Whitman stated, "I keep as delicate around the bowels as around the head and heart."

"The scent of these arm-pits," he wrote, was an "aroma finer than prayer."

Walt Whitman knew he had written poetry different from anything that had been written before. What would readers think of these long lines that did not rhyme or conform to careful meters? Would they understand his lists of occupations and body parts? The poems needed "some feet to stand on," Whitman decided. He included a preface in the book to explain the poems that followed.

"The poetic quality is not marshalled in rhyme or uniformity or abstract addresses," Whitman noted in his preface. Instead, it occurs naturally when a skilled poet brings together words and ideas. The music of poetry must develop freely, "as unerringly and loosely as lilacs or roses on a bush."

The greatest poet, stated the preface, is someone with "the ultimate brain." Whitman used the language of phrenology to describe that poet, explaining that he or she would possess "the soundest organic health, large hope and comparison, and fondness for women and children, large alimentiveness and destructiveness and causality, with a perfect sense of the oneness of nature."

Whitman viewed *Leaves of Grass* as a new Bible. His preface told not only how to read poetry, but how to live as well. "Love the earth and sun and the animals, despise riches," Whitman instructed, "read these leaves in the open air every season of every year of your life, re-examine all you have been told at school or church or in any book, dismiss whatever insults your own soul." If a reader lived this way, Whitman promised, "Your very flesh shall be a great poem."

Whitman printed 795 copies of *Leaves of Grass* and offered them for sale at the phrenology shop of Fowler and Wells. He advertised in the *New York Tribune*, making copies available for two dollars each. He gave away some copies and sent others to prominent Americans, including Ralph Waldo Emerson, the writer who had called for a great American poet.

And then on July 11, the proud author of the newly published book turned all his attention to his family. Walter Whitman, Sr., died on that day. Walt's sister Mary fell ill after the funeral. Walt escorted her to Greenport, on eastern Long Island, where she lived with her shipbuilder husband and their children.

Walt relaxed on the shore of Peconic Bay as Mary got well. He rode the Long Island Railroad back to Brooklyn, eager to return to work. He felt a "confirmed resolution," he stated, "from which I never afterwards wavered, to go on with my poetic enterprise in my own way, and finish it as well as I could."

But it appeared that Whitman's enterprise would not proceed smoothly. *Leaves of Grass* shocked most of the people who read it. One scholar said he "would be sorry to know that any woman had looked into it past the title-page."

Frank talk about the human body made many nineteenth-century Americans uncomfortable. They often behaved as if their bodies did not exist. Men covered themselves with long-sleeved jackets and long trousers. Women wore dresses with full skirts, garments that closed tightly around their necks and reached all the way to their shoes. These people considered it impolite to say the word *arm* or *leg* in mixed company. When they read Whitman's lines about bowels and wombs, armpits and sexuality, they could hardly believe their eyes!

Leaves of Grass received several nasty reviews in newspapers and magazines. "It is impossible to imagine how any man's fancy could have conceived such a mass of stupid filth," one reviewer wrote, "unless he were possessed of the soul of a sentimental donkey that had died of disappointed love." Another reviewer asked, "Who is this arrogant young man who proclaims himself Poet of Time, and who roots like a pig among the rotten garbage of licentious thoughts?"

GODEY'S "AMERICANISED" PARIS FASHIONS.

Nineteenth-century women wore clothes that covered nearly every part of the body.

PARIS, NEW YORK & PHILADELPHIA FASHIONS FOR SPRING AND SUMMER 1864, PUBLISHED & SOLD BY F. MAHAN, No 231 CHESNUT STREET, PHILADE

Fashionable dress for nineteenth-century men.

Most of the public, however, ignored the book. Copies of *Leaves of Grass* gathered dust on the shelves at Fowler and Wells's shop. Even Walt's own family showed little interest in his work. "I saw the book," recalled George Whitman. "Didn't read it at all—didn't think it worth reading."

His sister Hannah's husband, the well-educated Charles L. Heyde, dismissed Walt's book as being "irregular, disorderly, indifferent or defiant."

Walt was determined to drum up interest in his poems. He wrote his own reviews of *Leaves of Grass* and published them anonymously in the *American Phrenological Review* and other periodicals. He felt no shyness about praising himself or promoting his book. "Self-reliant, with haughty eyes, assuming to himself all the attributes of his country, steps Walt Whitman into literature, talking like a man unaware that there was ever hitherto such a production as a book, or such a being as a writer," the author wrote about himself. "Every word that falls from his mouth shows silent disdain and defiance of the old theories and forms. Every phrase announces new laws; not once do his lips unclose except in conformity with them."

Then Walt learned that someone else recognized the greatness of his work. Emerson wrote him a letter, praising Whitman's courage and original thinking. "I greet you at the beginning of a great career," Emerson said. *Leaves of Grass* was so astonishing that, he wrote, "I rubbed my eyes a little, to see if this sunbeam were no illusion."

Emerson speculated that anyone able to write a book with such depth and beauty "must have had a long foreground somewhere." He must have had years of instruction and practice writing poetry. Emerson touched upon a question that has puzzled many readers of Whitman's poems. How could a mediocre newspaper writer, someone who had shown no unusual talent, produce such outstanding poems? Even Whitman's years of intensive learning cannot account for the sudden appearance of his genius.

Sometime in the early 1850s, Whitman had had an insight. He had perceived a way to combine words and ideas that was altogether new. He saw how to do this with grace, simplicity, and deep feeling. He freed poets to write about the events of everyday life, and to create verses that were long or short, flowing or choppy, rhyming or not. Whitman's short book received little fanfare, but American poetry would never be the same again.

Knowing Emerson's letter could only draw attention to his book, Whitman made the most of it. He allowed it to be printed in the *Tribune* and other newspapers. And when he published a second edition of *Leaves of Grass*, in 1856, Emerson's words of praise shouted boldly from the book's spine in gold letters: "I greet you at the beginning of a great career."

The second edition contained twenty new poems, including "Crossing Brooklyn Ferry." Whitman gave a copy of the new *Leaves of Grass* to a friend of Emerson's, Henry David Thoreau. Thoreau visited Whitman in November 1856, along with another Massachusetts resident, Bronson Alcott, father of the author Louisa May Alcott.

Thoreau also had written a book that would become an American classic. His *Walden*, published in 1854, described a year spent in a cabin beside Walden Pond in Concord, Massachusetts. It challenged readers to simplify their lives, to get rid of all unnecessary possessions, and to drop activities that wasted their time. Thoreau urged people to seek experiences that would cause them to learn and grow.

Whitman appeared perfectly at ease entertaining guests in the bedroom he shared with his brother Eddy. He seemed not to notice the unmade bed or the chamber pot visible beneath it. After the meeting, Thoreau called Whitman a "great fellow." Thoreau admired the poems in *Leaves of Grass*, and he read them again and again. However, Whitman's openness in describing the human body offended the modest New Englander. "I think that men have not been ashamed of themselves without reason," Thoreau commented.

Whitman was already planning a third edition of *Leaves of Grass*, and within a year, he completed seventy-eight more poems. Whether there would be another *Leaves of Grass*, however, was in doubt. Sales of the first two editions had been poor. Needing money, Whitman went back to working for newspapers. He worried that he had no future as a poet. He wrote about himself, "Will he justify the great prophecy of Emerson? or will he too, like thousands of others, flaunt out one bright announcement, the result of gathered powers, only to sink back exhausted."

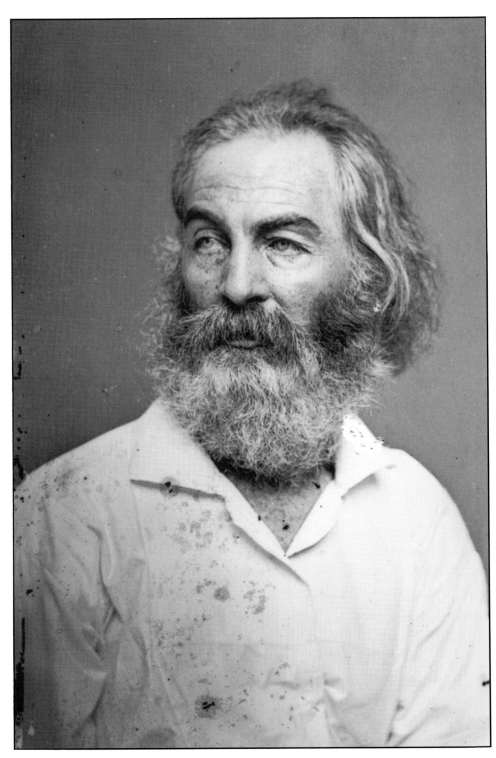

Walt Whitman in his forties.

CHAPTER SIX

Year of Forebodings

What am I myself but one of your meteors?

To WALT WHITMAN, 1860 was a "Year of meteors!" He wrote verses that sang about the year's events, happenings that flashed across the public's consciousness like a "strange huge meteor-procession dazzling and clear shooting over our heads . . ."

Edward, Prince of Wales, the future king of England, visited the United States in 1860 and paraded past crowds on Manhattan's avenues. The British steamship *Great Eastern*—six hundred feet in length—crossed the Atlantic for the first time and sailed into New York Bay. The Republican party nominated Abraham Lincoln, a lawyer from Illinois, to run for president.

But Whitman saw, too, that 1860 was a "year of forebodings!" The year 1859 had ended with the hanging death of John Brown, a zealous old man who had hoped to end slavery by force. Brown first gained national fame in 1856, when he and his sons killed five men in Kansas Territory.

The people of Kansas fought fiercely over the issue of owning slaves. Southern settlers wanted slavery to be legal in Kansas. Newcomers from the North insisted that slavery not spread to Kansas from the South. Many of the Northerners were abolitionists—people who wanted to make slavery illegal throughout the United States.

The men Brown killed had terrorized Kansas abolitionists and murdered several people. Brown saw himself as an avenger.

In October 1859, Brown and a group of followers seized the U.S. Arsenal, a storage place for guns and ammunition, in Harpers Ferry, Virginia (now in West Virginia). They hoped to inspire the African-American slaves in the region to revolt. U.S. forces, commanded by Robert E. Lee, surrounded the arsenal. The army captured Brown, who was tried and sentenced to death.

Most abolitionists employed peaceful methods for change, such as campaigning for antislavery laws. They made speeches and wrote books and articles describing the evils of slavery. Harriet Beecher Stowe's novel *Uncle Tom's Cabin*, published in 1852, was one of the strongest condemnations of slavery. It sold a half million copies in five years and converted many men and women to abolitionism. Some abolitionists helped slaves escape to Canada via the secret network known as the Underground Railroad.

Although many Americans in the North and South looked upon John Brown as a fanatic, the abolitionists called him a hero. They praised him as a martyr to the cause of human freedom. To Henry David Thoreau, for example, Brown was "a man such as the sun may not rise upon again in this benighted land."

Walt Whitman, in contrast, reacted warily to the news of John Brown's raid and capture. He feared that such militancy on the part of abolitionists could lead the nation into war. "If things go on at this rate," he jotted in his notebook, "the Union is threatened with a destiny horrible as it is altogether a novelty, something that never happened to any nation before—it is likely to be saved to death."

Perhaps the abolitionists were willing to tear apart their nation to end slavery. Whitman preferred to let slavery continue in the places where it was established rather than destroy the United States of America. Like most people in the North, Whitman considered the abolitionists to be extremists. Even Abraham Lincoln, the presidential candidate most committed to equality for the races, never promised to abolish slavery. Lincoln called the practice of slaveholding "an evil not to be extended," and he believed it would die out with time.

The Last Moments of John Brown, *a painting by Thomas Hovenden.*

Lincoln's Picture
one of the latest taken
before he was shot —
the most satisfactory
picture of A. L. I have
ever seen, (and I have seen
hundreds of different ones) — Looks
just like I saw him last on the balcony
of the National Hotel

Keep Careful

ABRAHAM LINCOLN.

Whitman's favorite picture of Abraham Lincoln. "Looks just like I saw him last on the balcony of the National Hotel," the poet wrote on the back of it.

Presidential politics, the debate over slavery, a royal visit, technological progress—1860 was a "year all mottled with evil and good," Whitman concluded. It was a "Year of comets and meteors transient and strange," and Whitman asked, "What am I myself but one of your meteors?" Bad fortune and good affected his life as well. He weathered the discouragement of poor book sales and bad reviews. Then he received a letter from Boston, Massachusetts, and his emotions soared. The publishing firm of Thayer and Eldridge wanted to print *Leaves of Grass*.

In their letter, William Thayer and Charles Eldridge, the firm's young owners, wrote, "When the book was first issued we were clerks in the establishment we now own. We read the book with profit and pleasure. It is a true poem and writ by a *true* man." The letter promised, "we can and will sell a large number of copies."

In March 1860, a month after the letter arrived, Walt was in Boston, setting type and correcting page proofs for the new edition of his book. Thayer and Eldridge gave him free rein in their printshop, trusting him to make all of the decisions about the book's content and appearance.

Whitman had been only too glad to give up journalism. He had no interest in Brooklyn's sewers, the new hobby of keeping home aquariums, or any of the other topics he wrote about for the dailies. And he recognized that he lacked the personality for newspaper work. "My opinions are all, always, so hazy," he commented. "I am no use in any situation which calls for instant decision."

In Boston, Walt stayed in a rented room and ate his meals in restaurants. He complained about the high cost of food in a letter to his brother Jeff: "7 cents for a cup of coffee and 19 cents for a beefsteak—*and me so fond of coffee and beefsteak!*"

Emerson traveled from Concord to visit Whitman in Boston. The two men walked for hours under the elms on Boston Common, a public gathering place, deep in discussion. Emerson was worried that some of the more shocking lines in *Leaves of Grass* would keep the

Properly dressed Bostonians liked to socialize near the Brewer Fountain on Boston Common.

book from selling well. He urged Whitman to expurgate, or remove, all mention of the human body and sexuality from his poems.

Expurgation would diminish the quality of his work, Whitman believed, and he refused to do that. "If I had cut sex out, I might just as well have cut everything out," he said. Also, Whitman objected to the idea that there was anything immoral in his poetry. "Expurgation is apology," he explained years later, "an admission that something or other was wrong. Emerson said expurgate—I said no, no. . . . I have not lived to regret my Emerson no.''

Whitman summed up his opinion this way: "The dirtiest book in all the world is the expurgated book." His verses would be printed as he had written them.

Bostonians had reacted strongly to the first two editions of *Leaves of Grass*. "Woe and shame for the Land of Liberty if its literature's stream is thus to flow from the filthy fountains of licentious corruption!" wrote a reviewer in the *Boston Post*. "Both Whitman's *Leaves* and Emerson's laudation had a common origin in temporary insanity."

New England society was known for strict morals and proper dress, stemming from its Puritan roots. It seemed to Walt that Boston functioned under a "cramper." He felt conspicuous, but happily so, wearing rough clothes and trousers tucked into his boots. "Everybody here is so like everybody else—and I am Walt Whitman!" he observed.

This city of prudish attitudes and behavior was one of the most outspoken places in the nation when it came to opposing slavery. The abolitionist movement was born in Boston in 1831, when William Lloyd Garrison founded an antislavery newspaper, the *Liberator*. In Boston, Whitman saw a city where African Americans had more freedom and mobility than they had in New York. He saw blacks setting type in printshops, working as lawyers, and serving on juries. Black customers were free to sit among whites in restaurants.

Thayer and Eldridge had recently published an antislavery novel, *Harrington*, by a young writer named William Douglas O'Connor. Whitman met O'Connor at the publishers' office and liked him immediately, although some of O'Connor's opinions troubled him. "I remember I fear'd his ardent abolitionism—was afraid it would probably keep us apart," Whitman said.

O'Connor felt no qualms about accepting Whitman as a friend, despite their differing ideas. He expressed his admiration of the poet freely, writing, "He is so large & strong—so pure, proud, & tender, with such an ineffable *bon-hommie* & wholesome sweetness of presence . . ."

Walt wrote to Jeff again when the new edition of *Leaves of Grass* had been published. The book, "in the permanent form it now is, looks as well and reads as well (to my own notion) as I anticipated," he wrote, "because a good deal, after all, was an experiment—and now I am satisfied."

Whitman modeled one of his poetic experiments after the operas that he loved. In "Out of the Cradle Endlessly Rocking," he traveled back in time to his childhood. He imagined himself as a child on the beaches of Paumanok, or Long Island, "When the lilac-scent was in the air and Fifth-month grass was growing."

Each day the child came to the beach and watched two mockingbirds, "Two feather'd guests from Alabama," care for the spotted eggs in their nest, Whitman wrote. Then, one day, the female bird was gone. Her sorrowful mate expressed his grief in arias—songlike stanzas filled with deep emotion.

> O brown halo in the sky near the moon, drooping upon the sea!
> O troubled reflection in the sea!
> O throat! O throbbing heart!
> And I singing uselessly, uselessly all the night.

As the bird sang without ceasing and scanned the horizon for its lost love, the ocean waves washed rhythmically onto the shore like an accompanying orchestra. The waves whispered, "Death, death, death, death, death."

The earth, in Whitman's poem, was a great cradle, endlessly bringing forth new life. Yet the cradle rocked to the tempo of the never-ending tide of death.

Like "Song of Myself," this new poem described the cycle of birth and death. Individuals are born and sing their songs of joy or sadness, as the mockingbird did, only to return in death to the cradle from which all life springs. And just as the child of an earlier poem ab-

sorbed sights and sounds, the boy of this poem absorbed the mockingbird's song and was forever changed.

The boy realized his destiny was to be a poet. He would sing his
own "responsive songs," made sweeter and stronger by the presence
of "the low and delicious word death."

The new poems in *Leaves of Grass* praised the states of the Union,
which Whitman called "Democracy's lands." Whitman gave voice
to his concern for the future of the nation: "And I will make a song
that there shall be comity by day and by night between all the States,
and between any two of them . . ."

Some of the poems added to the book in 1860 make it apparent
that Whitman was homosexual. They celebrate "manly attachment"
and "athletic love." In the poem "A Glimpse," for example, Whitman took his readers into a barroom on a winter night. He showed
them:

> . . . *a youth who loves me and whom I love, silently approaching*
> *and seating himself near, that he may hold me by the hand,*
> *A long while amid the noises of coming and going, of drinking and*
> *oath and smutty jest,*
> *There we two, content, happy in being together, speaking little,*
> *perhaps not a word.*

Homosexuality was poorly understood in Whitman's time. Many
people had no idea that it was possible for someone to feel attracted
to members of his or her own sex. Lines such as these were less
shocking to Whitman's readers than were his mention of human
body parts. Most nineteenth-century men and women saw in these
lines a description of male friendship.

His work in Boston finished, Whitman returned to Brooklyn. He
spent most of his evenings in Pfaff's beer cellar, a Manhattan gathering place for writers. As the regulars traded gossip and jokes, Whitman sat apart listening, sipping beer, and eating German sausages.
"My own greatest pleasure at Pfaff's was to look on—to see, talk

little, absorb," Whitman noted. "I never was a great discusser anyway."

William Dean Howells, a young man from Ohio just starting his writing career, met Walt Whitman at Pfaff's in 1860. Howells remembered that the poet "leaned back in his chair, and reached out his great hand to me, as if he were going to give it to me for good and all." Howells would go on to write several novels and books about literature. He would help Mark Twain, Stephen Crane, and other American writers advance their careers. The memory of meeting Walt Whitman would stay with him in detail—Whitman's apparent strength, gray hair and beard, "and gentle eyes that looked most kindly into mine, and seemed to wish the liking which I instantly gave him, though we hardly passed a word."

Whitman's warm gaze impressed many people who met him. Soon after returning to New York, he received a letter from William Thayer, one of his publishers in Boston. Walt's Boston friends missed him, Thayer wrote, and wished he would return to their city. Thayer wrote that Walt's friend William O'Connor longed "for the privilege of looking into those eyes of calm, and through them to enter into that soul, so deep in its emotions, so majestic in all its thought-movements, and yet so simple and childlike."

Thayer and Eldridge had promised to sell a large number of copies of *Leaves of Grass*. But before the year ended, their publishing firm went out of business. Sales of the 1860 edition earned Whitman only $250. His meteoric flash of success seemed to have burned itself out.

Whitman had no idea that interest in his work was kindling across the Atlantic Ocean. The painter and poet William Bell Scott had bought a secondhand copy of *Leaves of Grass* in London. Scott showed the book to his friends, including Dante Gabriel Rossetti, a prominent poet and artist. The London readers saw greatness in Whitman's poems and recognized their author as a "very original and extraordinary genius."

Few Americans, however, had time to ponder the merits of a book of poems as 1860 drew to a close. Their nation faced a crisis. In November, Abraham Lincoln was elected president. Many citizens rejoiced. Walt Whitman saw in Lincoln an ideal leader, a "Redeemer President of these States." In 1856, Whitman had written a political pamphlet, *The Eighteenth Presidency!* He had called for "some heroic, shrewd, fully-informed, healthy-bodied, middle-aged, beard-faced American" to "come down from the West across the Alleghanies, and walk into the Presidency . . ." Lincoln appeared to be that man.

Other Americans mourned the election of Lincoln. The *Dallas Herald* lamented that "evil days" had arrived. The leadership of South Carolina, convinced that Lincoln would abolish slavery, announced that their state was seceding, or leaving the Union.

The president-elect traveled to Washington, D.C., in early 1861 to take command of a nation falling apart. It was a greater task, he said, than the one that had faced President George Washington. Lincoln had received threats on his life. Still, he made numerous stops on his twelve-day train trip to the capital, giving speeches and greeting crowds.

More than thirty thousand New Yorkers stopped traffic on Broadway when Lincoln came to Manhattan. They stood on tiptoe and stretched their necks to get a peek at the man they had elected.

From his spot at the top of a bus, Walt Whitman had a "capital" view of the goings-on, he said. He saw Lincoln step out of the coach that had carried him from the train to the Astor House. On this day, there were no speeches or cheers. Lincoln looked at the crowd for several moments, then turned and entered the hotel.

Whitman observed Lincoln's appearance and mannerisms, "his perfect composure and coolness—his unusual and uncouth height, his dress of complete black, stovepipe hat push'd back on the head." Whitman remarked that Lincoln "look'd with curiosity upon that immense sea of faces, and the sea of faces return'd the look with similar curiosity."

On March 4, Lincoln stood outside the U.S. Capitol to take the Oath of Office. The unfinished Capitol dome symbolized the fractured nature of the United States. Mississippi, Alabama, Georgia, Louisiana, Texas, and Florida had joined South Carolina in secession.

Whitman attended many operas at the Academy of Music on Fourteenth Street in Manhattan.

These seven states had formed their own nation, the Confederate States of America. Four more slaveholding states—Tennessee, Virginia, North Carolina, and Arkansas—would soon join them.

Lincoln promised that under his leadership the American people would see "the laws of the Union be faithfully executed in all the States." Lincoln's predecessor, President James Buchanan, had done nothing to stop the Southern states from seceding. Now Lincoln implored the Confederates to return to the United States peacefully. He did not want war. But he refused to do nothing and prove that a great experiment in democracy—the United States of America—had failed.

On the evening of April 12, Walt Whitman attended an opera at the Academy of Music on Fourteenth Street in Manhattan. It was

A Confederate photographer took this picture of the damage at Fort Sumter.

nearly midnight when he left the opera house and walked along Broadway toward the Brooklyn Ferry. Even in 1861, Manhattan's busy streets never slept, and Whitman loved to be part of the bustle and noise. Coaches rattled over the cobblestones. Strolling men and women laughed and chatted under the gaslights. Boys hawking papers called out "Extra!" to passersby.

On this night, the boys were agitated, hurrying along the sidewalks and shouting. Walt bought a newspaper. And when he read the headline, he learned that his worst fears for the United States had been realized. Before dawn, Confederate forces had opened fire on Fort Sumter, an army installation in the harbor of Charleston, South Carolina. Whitman's joy in the nighttime city evaporated. War had arrived.

People in many Northern cities cheered the soldiers going off to war. Here, the citizens of Detroit watch as the men of the 1st Michigan Infantry receive their flags on May 1, 1861.

CHAPTER SEVEN

Soldiers' Missionary

I sit by the restless all the dark night, some are so young,
Some suffer so much, I recall the experience sweet and sad . . .

A FEVER OF PATRIOTISM spread through towns and cities in the North. Following the bombardment of Fort Sumter, President Lincoln had called for seventy-five thousand new soldiers to serve in the army for three months. Like most people in the North, Lincoln believed the war to reunite the nation would soon end in victory. Young men hurried to enlist as soldiers. In New York and in other cities, crowds cheered the new regiments as they left for the battle lines.

In Brooklyn, Walt Whitman saw newly mustered soldiers march off to war with pieces of rope tied to the barrels of their rifles. The ropes were "to bring back each man a prisoner from the audacious South, to be led in a noose, on our men's early and triumphant return!" Whitman explained.

He felt electrified during the first few weeks of the war, and he conveyed his excitement in the poem "First O Songs for a Prelude":

> *The blood of the city up—arm'd! arm'd! the cry everywhere,*
> *The flags flung out from the steeples of churches and from all*
> *   the public buildings and stores,*
> *The tearful parting, the mother kisses her son, the son kisses*
> *   his mother . . .*

. . . . . .
The tumultuous escort, the ranks of policemen preceding,
    clearing the way,
The unpent enthusiasm, the wild cheers of the crowd for their
    favorites . . .

George Whitman enlisted in the 51st New York Regiment. He signed on for one hundred days as a militia private, but would remain in the army for four long years. Walt, in spite of his strong support for the Union cause, had no intention of joining the army. "I could never think of myself as firing a gun or drawing a sword on another man," he explained.

Walt had been volunteering in a Manhattan hospital, caring for sick and injured coach drivers. By the spring of 1862, he was nursing wounded soldiers as well. The number of casualties from battle had been high. The military had filled an entire wing at one New York hospital.

It soon became clear that a Union victory would be neither swift nor easy. In the first battle of the war, fought on July 21, 1861, Union and Confederate armies met near a Virginia creek called Bull Run. Confused and stunned by the brutality of war, the Union soldiers retreated in chaos, allowing the smaller Southern force to win the battle. Disappointed Northerners referred to the conflict at Bull Run as "the great skedaddle."

Walt Whitman felt the loss deeply, and he feared for his nation's future. "The dream of humanity, the vaunted Union we thought so strong, so impregnable—lo! it seems already smash'd like a china plate." He called the loss at Bull Run "one bitter, bitter hour," and he hoped that "proud America will never again know such an hour."

Another Union retreat followed the Peninsular Campaign of 1862. General George McClellan led an army of one hundred thousand men into the strip of land that separates the York and James rivers of Virginia. McClellan had planned to attack Richmond, capital of the Confederacy. But when he reached the outskirts of the

George Whitman sat for a photographer in his soldier's uniform.

The New York soldiers led by General Louis Blenker stayed at their posts during the panic at Bull Run.

city, he hesitated. He worried that his troops would be outnumbered, and he called for reinforcements.

McClellan's caution gave Robert E. Lee time to move a large fighting force to Richmond. Lee, the military leader who had captured John Brown, was now a Confederate general. The soldiers commanded by McClellan and Lee fought the Battle of the Seven Days between June 25 and July 1. Although neither side won decisively, McClellan's men turned and headed north.

General McClellan hesitated again after the bloody battle near Antietam Creek in Maryland. More soldiers—both Union and Confederate—died at Antietam on September 17, 1862, than on any other day of the war. McClellan welcomed thirteen thousand new soldiers on the morning following the battle. Lincoln wanted him to launch a fresh attack on Lee's army and perhaps end the war. But McClellan allowed Lee's men to slip across the Potomac River into Virginia.

McClellan's failure to act troubled Lincoln. However, the president looked upon the Battle of Antietam as a Union victory, a sign that God wanted the North to win the war. Lincoln issued the Emancipation Proclamation. This document granted freedom to the slaves in Confederate-held territory, effective January 1, 1863. With the Emancipation Proclamation, the Civil War became a struggle to repair the Union—and to free the slaves.

The two armies met again at Fredericksburg, Virginia, in December 1862. This encounter was clearly a Confederate victory. Led by General Ambrose Burnside, the Union's Army of the Potomac had constructed a pontoon bridge—one designed to float—across the Rappahannock River. Burnside's force of 113,000 crossed the bridge and entered the town of Fredericksburg, near Washington, D.C. The Union men then attacked Lee's army, which was positioned on hills to the west and south of town.

The assault failed, and the Rebels drove the Union army back, killing or wounding more than twelve thousand. The Confederate casualties numbered fewer than five thousand. Injured, bleeding men lay on the ground through the freezing night. In the morning, the two sides called a truce to bury their dead. Then the Army of the Potomac limped back across the river.

At home in Brooklyn, Walt Whitman read about the loss at Fredericksburg in a newspaper. The paper listed the names of men who had been wounded in the battle, and George Whitman's name was on the list. Walt wasted no time. He boarded a train and set off to find his brother.

Sick and wounded soldiers await medical treatment at Savage Station, Virginia.

Burying the dead after the battle at Fredericksburg.

It was a distressing trip for Walt even before he reached his destination. He had his pocket picked while he was changing trains in Philadelphia, Pennsylvania, and he arrived penniless in Washington, D.C. As he roamed the city on foot, trying to get news of George, Walt endured "the greatest suffering I ever experienced in my life," he wrote, "walking all day and night, unable to ride, trying to get information, trying to get access to big people, &c—I could not get the least clue to anything."

Washington, situated on the border of the Confederacy, was a city disrupted by war. Trains arrived one after another. Some brought newly enlisted soldiers into the capital. Others carried wounded and sick men who were bound for the city's hospitals. Runaway slaves seeking freedom poured into the city as well.

The army baked bread for its soldiers in the basement of the U.S. Capitol, and issued uniforms at the Corcoran Gallery of Art. Cattle grazed on the White House grounds. They would be butchered to feed hungry troops. Soldiers tramped past the Capitol, with its unfinished dome, and the Washington Monument, a project abandoned before it was completed.

Two of Whitman's Boston friends, the writer William O'Connor and the publisher Charles Eldridge, had taken wartime jobs with the government in Washington. Walt finally asked them for help. Both friends loaned him money. O'Connor learned that George's unit was camped in Falmouth, Virginia, and obtained a military pass for Walt to travel there.

George had only received a cut on his cheek during the battle. Walt was relieved to find his brother well, but he was deeply distressed at the death and misery he saw in the army camp. Wounded men filled the hospital tents at Falmouth. Amputated arms and legs lay in piles, "cut, bloody, black and blue, swelling and sickening," Walt said.

Union soldiers occupying the grounds of the U.S. Capitol.

For the first time, Walt clearly understood "what sick men and mangled men endure." He witnessed death, and he recorded images of the dead in poetry. These lines are from a poem titled "A Sight in Camp in the Daybreak Gray and Dim":

> *Three forms I see on stretchers lying, brought out there*
>   *untended lying,*
> *Over each the blanket spread, ample brownish woolen blanket . . .*
> *. . . . .*
> *Then with light fingers I from the face of the nearest the first*
>   *just lift the blanket;*
> *Who are you elderly man so gaunt and grim, with well-gray'd hair,*
>   *and flesh all sunken about the eyes?*
> *. . . . .*
> *Then to the second I step—and who are you my child and*
>   *darling?*
> *. . . . .*
> *Then to the third—a face nor child nor old, very calm, as of*
>   *beautiful yellow-white ivory;*
> *Young man I think I know you—I think this face is the face*
>   *of the Christ himself . . .*

Whitman visited Fredericksburg, scene of the recent battle, and recorded his observations in a notebook, planning to work them into a poem later on. "Splintered, bursted, crumbled, the houses—some with their chimneys thrown down—the hospitals—the man with his mouth blown out," he quickly wrote.

Walt stayed with George for more than a week, sharing his tent and his food. He had seen the reality of war, and his outlook was forever changed. "Now that I have lived for 8 or 9 days amid such scenes as the camps furnish," he wrote to his mother, "really nothing we call trouble seems worth talking about." Walt knew that he belonged among the troops. He would do what he could to help and comfort them.

He had learned from Thoreau, whose book he was reading, how to live a simple life. He would put Thoreau's lessons into practice. "I can be satisfied and happy henceforward if I can get one meal a day, and know that mother and all are in good health," he decided.

On December 28, Walt left George and returned to Washington, D.C. He rented a room at the corner of Fourteenth and L streets, and Charles Eldridge helped him get a part-time job at the Army Paymaster's Office. Whitman applied for a full-time position with the government, but he had no offers. He looked nothing like an office worker, and many officials refused to hire a man in rough clothes and a shaggy beard. "You look for all the world, like an old Southern planter—a regular Carolina or Virginia planter," Senator Preston King of New York told Whitman.

Walt also failed to find work for another reason: He didn't look very hard. He spent most of his free time nursing ill and wounded soldiers.

More than forty military hospitals had been established in Washington, wherever the army could find space. Sick men filled beds in churches and in schools. Even the U.S. Patent Office now housed a hospital. Whitman served as a volunteer for the U.S. Christian Commission, a group devoted to meeting the needs of the Union army. Inside the cover of his notebook he wrote, "Walt Whitman—Soldiers' Missionary."

Each day, after finishing work at the paymaster's office, Whitman stopped at home to bathe and change his clothes. Then he hurried to one of the hospitals to visit the soldiers, men and boys he called "my own children or younger brothers."

Like the other Civil War nurses, most of whom were men, Whitman cleaned and bandaged wounds and helped with amputations. If a soldier had been shot in the arm or the leg, doctors often removed the limb before an infection could set in. There were no antibiotics to kill germs at that time, and an infection could mean death. Many times, Whitman held the hand of a frightened soldier while the painful operation took place.

Soldiers who lost limbs in battle were among the people gathered at the headquarters of the U.S. Christian Commission.

The patients of Ward K, Armory Square Hospital.

Whitman described some of his nursing duties in a moving poem titled "The Wound-Dresser":

Bearing the bandages, water and sponge,
Straight and swift to my wounded I go . . .
. . . .
To each and all one after another I draw near, not one do I
*   miss,*
An attendant follows holding a tray, he carries a refuse pail,
Soon to be fill'd with clotted rags and blood, emptied, and
*   fill'd again.*

Concerned that "the real war will never get into the books," Whitman spared no bloody detail when describing the wounded.

The neck of the cavalry-man with the bullet through and through
*   I examine,*
Hard the breathing rattles, quite glazed already the eye, yet
*   life struggles hard . . .*
. . . . . .
From the stump of the arm, the amputated hand,
I undo the clotted lint, remove the slough, wash off the matter
*   and blood . . .*
. . . .
I dress the perforated shoulder, the foot with the bullet-wound,
Cleanse the one with a gnawing and putrid gangrene, so
*   sickening, so offensive . . .*

Whitman liked to bring small gifts to his patients, to make their suffering a little more bearable. He passed out oranges, tobacco, writing paper, and candy. Once, he paid a woman to cook rice pudding for a sick soldier who craved it. On a hot summer day, he brought ice cream to the men in one ward. Whitman asked acquaintances in New York and Massachusetts for funds to pay for these trifles, and many complied. Still, he wrote to his mother that there was never enough money "to do the good I would like to do—& the work grows upon me."

Walt wrote to Martha Whitman, Jeff's wife, about his visits to the soldiers. "O my dear sister, how your heart would ache to go through the rows of wounded young men, as I did," he said in his letter. He told of one young man who was very ill and who had received no medical attention. Walt sent for a doctor, who examined the soldier and said he would recover. The soldier had severe diarrhea, a common ailment in both armies of the Civil War, and bronchitis.

Whitman sat and talked with the young man for a long time. "He seemed to have entirely give up, and lost heart—he had not a cent of money—not a friend or acquaintance," Whitman continued. He told his sister-in-law that he had given the youth some change to buy milk. "Trifling as this was," Walt said, "he was overcome and began to cry."

The "Soldiers' Missionary" estimated that he made more than six hundred visits to the hospitals and aided between eighty thousand and one hundred thousand men. He wrote many letters to the loved ones of the hospitalized soldiers. He chatted with the convalescing men and entertained them with games of "twenty questions." He sat beside them when they slept. At times he held them while they died. "I sit by the restless all the dark night, some are so young," he wrote in "The Wound-Dresser," "Some suffer so much, I recall the experience sweet and sad . . ."

Even when he left the hospitals, Whitman saw the tragic results of war. Processions of ambulances—crude, horse-drawn wagons—carried suffering men away from the city's wharves. The men had been loaded onto boats after battle for transportation to Washington's hospitals. There were times when it seemed to Whitman that the entire United States was now "one vast central hospital."

President Lincoln, out for a ride, was also a common sight on Washington's streets, and Whitman bowed politely to him when they passed. Whitman compared Lincoln's leadership in wartime to a sea captain navigating in a storm. "He has shown, I sometimes

Whitman saved this photograph of Will Wallace, one of the many soldiers he befriended in Washington's hospitals.

Washington
June 10, 1865.

Mr. & Mrs. Pratt;

As I am visiting your son Alfred occasionally, to cheer him up in his sickness in hospital, I thought you might like a few words, though from a stranger, yet a friend to your boy. I was there last night, and sat a while by the bed, as usual, & he showed me the letter he had just received from home. He wrote to you yesterday. He has had diarrhea pretty bad, but is now improved & goes about the hospital — but as the weather is pretty hot & powerful in the midst of the day, I advised him not to go out doors much at present. What he wants most is rest, and a chance to get his strength again. I expect he will

Whitman often wrote letters to the wounded soldiers' loved ones.

We are having very hot weather here, & it is dry & dusty.— The City is alive with soldiers from both the Army of the Potomac & the Western Armies, brought here by Sherman. There have been some great Reviews here, as you have seen in the papers — & thousands of soldiers are going home every day.

You must write to Alfred often, as it cheers up a boy sick & away from home. Write all about domestic & farm incidents, and as cheerful as may be. Direct to him, in Ward C, Armory Square Hospital, Washington, D.C. Should any thing occur, I will write you again, but I feel confident he will continue doing well. For the present farewell.

Walt Whitman
Washington
D C

think, an almost supernatural tact in keeping the ship afloat at all," Whitman said, "with head steady, not only not going down, and now certain not to, but with proud and resolute spirit, and flag flying in sight of the world, menacing and high as ever."

On Sundays, Whitman dined with William O'Connor and his wife, Nelly. Nelly O'Connor often cooked roast beef, one of Walt's favorite meals. The conversation usually turned to the war after dinner, and it tended to grow heated. William O'Connor was still a confirmed abolitionist. He wanted an end to slavery regardless of the cost in human life.

Whitman's experiences in the hospitals had led him to a different point of view. "My opinion is *to stop the war now*," he said. As he explained, wars were "about nine hundred and ninety-nine parts diarrhea to one part glory: the people who like the wars should be compelled to fight the wars." More than once, the arguments grew so loud that the O'Connors' neighbors summoned the police.

Another close friend to Whitman during the war years was John Burroughs, a teacher from New York. Burroughs had come to Washington to work for the United States Treasury Department. He would later gain fame as a naturalist and writer. Burroughs taught Whitman about the wildlife living in the eastern woodlands and marshes. Whitman especially liked Burroughs's description of the hermit thrush, a bird known for its beautiful singing. Burroughs called the thrush's song "the voice of that calm, sweet solemnity one attains to in his best moments."

Whitman impressed the young Burroughs with his broad range of interests, his expressive gaze, and his honest affection for others. "The more I see and talk with him, the greater he becomes to me," Burroughs said. "He loves everything and everybody."

Only his family could draw Whitman away from Washington and the soldiers. In the fall of 1863, he began receiving letters that told about trouble at home. Walt's sister Hannah was in poor health. Jesse Whitman was showing signs of mental illness. Andrew Whitman, thirty-six years old, was dying of tuberculosis and alcoholism. "Un-

President Lincoln visited his officers at Sharpsburg, Maryland, site of the Battle of Antietam.

Walt Whitman in 1863.

less you come home quite soon," Jeff wrote to Walt, "you certainly will never see Andrew alive."

With his father dead and Jesse ill, Walt acted as head of the Whitman family. He went home to Brooklyn in early November and stayed there until December 1. He did his best to appear calm and hopeful to his loved ones, but their situation upset him greatly. Prone to violence, Jesse had to be restrained from attacking his relatives. (Walt would have him committed to a mental institution within a year.) The dying Andrew's family lived in poverty and filth. Walt wished he could afford a cottage for his mother on Long Island. He wished he could move her away from the problems she faced every day.

Andrew died two days after Walt returned to Washington. Andrew's wife, Nancy, left with three children, no income, and a drinking problem of her own, turned to prostitution. Worry and grief occupied Walt's thoughts. "Mother, I think about you all more than ever—& poor Andrew, I often think about him," Whitman wrote in a letter.

Walt had always bragged about his rugged good health. But by the spring of 1864, the stress caused by his family and the war began to take a toll. He went to Brooklyn for a visit in June, just after his forty-fifth birthday. He arrived "in the character of a man not entirely well," Jeff Whitman said. Jeff observed that Walt was "not so unconsciously hearty as before."

Walt suffered from spells of dizziness and weakness. He had trouble falling asleep at night. Much of the time, he felt depressed. "It is awful to see so much, & not be able to relieve it," he wrote.

The fighting at Gettysburg destroyed trees, fences, and livestock.

CHAPTER EIGHT

Black, Black, Black

O how shall I warble myself for the dead one there I loved?
And how shall I deck my song for the large sweet soul
that has gone?

AFTER THREE YEARS of war, men were still killing and maiming one another on America's battlefields. But the character of the war had changed. Some key battles had given the Union an advantage.

In June 1863, General Robert E. Lee had marched his army north into Pennsylvania. Union troops met the Confederates in the small town of Gettysburg on July 1. The Northern and Southern forces fought brutally at Gettysburg over three sweltering days.

When the gunfire ceased, dead and bleeding men littered the town's fields and orchards. The Union counted twenty-three thousand men killed, wounded, or missing. Confederate losses were higher—as many as twenty-eight thousand men. The South lost seventeen generals and a third of Lee's fighting force. With almost no ammunition left, the Rebels retreated during a July 4 rainstorm. The Confederate army would never again try to fight on Union soil.

As the defeated Southerners withdrew from Pennsylvania, the Union general Ulysses S. Grant scored another victory to the west. Grant captured the river town of Vicksburg, Mississippi, after a forty-seven-day assault. Seizing Vicksburg meant the Union gained control of the Mississippi River, an important shipping route. And because the great river flowed through the heart of the South, Grant had weakened the Confederate nation by dividing it in two.

The Union followed its victories with a push into Tennessee, Alabama, and Georgia. Northern military units burned the city of Atlanta, Georgia. They destroyed crops, supplies, and buildings— anything that might help their enemy sustain its war effort.

The American people reelected President Abraham Lincoln in 1864. Lincoln took the Oath of Office for the second time in March 1865. The war was coming to an end. And as the sun broke through clouds over the U.S. Capitol, Lincoln started the work of healing America's war wounds. He urged people "to care for him who shall have borne the battle, and for his widow, and his orphan—to do all which may achieve and cherish a just, and a lasting peace, among ourselves, and with all nations."

Walt Whitman watched Lincoln return to the White House after the inauguration. He saw how the war had strained and aged the president, just as it had harmed his own health. Lincoln looked "very much worn and tired," Whitman said. "The lines, indeed, of vast responsibilities, intricate questions, and demands of life and death, cut deeper than ever upon his dark brown face." Whitman could see, however, "all the old goodness, tenderness, sadness, and canny shrewdness, underneath the furrows."

Lincoln's Second Inaugural Ball was held in the United States Patent Office, previously the site of a Civil War hospital. Whitman contrasted the present gaiety with the scenes of suffering that had occupied the same space just months earlier: "To-night, beautiful women, perfumes, the violins' sweetness, the polka and the waltz; then the amputation, the blue face, the groan, the glassy eye of the dying, the clotted rag, the odor of wounds and blood, and many a mother's son amid strangers, passing away untended there."

The bearded nurse who made those comments was now a full-time government worker. In January, Whitman had started working as a clerk in the Office of Indian Affairs, a division of the Interior Department. He was paid twelve hundred dollars a year to copy reports and documents. Walt felt relieved to have found a job, but he soon fell into the lazy work habits of his Brooklyn days. "I take things very easy," he wrote in a letter to Jeff. "The rule is to come at 9 and go at 4—but I don't come at 9, and only stay till 4 when I want."

Walt refused to let his job take time away from his visits to the soldiers. Also, he needed time to finish a writing project. He had written a group of poems during the Civil War. The poems described the thrilling first weeks of the war, when young men marched off to battle filled with optimism. They presented scenes of camp life, and listed the painful duties of a wartime nurse. Whitman's poetry depicted soldiers marching over the countryside and wading across streams. It recounted events of battles that wounded men had described.

In one poem, Whitman imagined a soldier's family receiving a letter—a letter written by a nurse, someone like himself. His lines captured the family's shock and worry.

> *O this is not our son's writing, yet his name is sign'd,*
> *O a strange hand writes for our dear son, O stricken mother's*
>   *soul!*
> *All swims before her eyes, flashes with black, she catches*
>   *the main words only,*
> *Sentences broken,* gunshot wound in the breast, cavalry
>   skirmish, taken to hospital . . .

The family in the poem tried to be hopeful. The letter told them their boy would recover. Meanwhile, the letter writer knew the sad truth, news that the family would receive all too soon: "The only son is dead."

Whitman arranged for a New York company to print *Drum-Taps*, a small book of his Civil War poems. He took a leave of absence from his job in early April, and went to Brooklyn to visit his mother and to supervise the printing.

He left behind warm days and budding flowers. Spring had arrived early in Washington that year. By April 1, lilac bushes were in full bloom. Their heart-shaped leaves and fragrant blossoms shaded porches throughout the capital. Migrating birds had returned to the swamps at the nearby Potomac River's edge. They sang noisily throughout the day as they built their nests. With the coming of summer's humidity, clouds would often cover Washington. But in early spring, there were still many clear, starry nights. Whitman had noticed Venus shining brightly in the evening sky.

On April 9, Walt and Louisa Whitman heard a chorus of church bells. Word had reached Brooklyn that in the small settlement of Appomattox Courthouse, Virginia, General Robert E. Lee had surrendered to the Union commander Ulysses S. Grant. The Civil War had ended.

The war had claimed the lives of 620,000 men. More than that number had been wounded. The United States had emerged from the ordeal as a single, strong nation, and all of the slaves were now free.

The bells tolled again on April 15. This time, they rang in mourning. President Lincoln was dead, assassinated by the actor John Wilkes Booth. Walt Whitman felt deep sorrow upon hearing the news. To him, Lincoln was the savior of democracy, the greatest hero of the American Civil War. "By many has this Union been help'd," Whitman wrote, "but if one name, one man, must be pick'd out, he, most of all, is the conservator of it, to the future."

Just as modern people stay close to their televisions and radios during times of crisis, Walt and Louisa Whitman bought newspapers throughout the day. The morning and evening papers printed several "extras," or special editions. Whitman searched the columns of print for details of the tragic story.

Neither son nor mother had any appetite. Louisa Whitman usually cooked hearty meals for Walt on his visits home—pancakes for breakfast, broiled fish, and homemade bread. On this day, their food sat on the table uneaten. They drank only a little coffee.

Walt left the house for a while to walk alone on Broadway. Rain soaked his clothes and struck his face when he looked up at the sky. The black clouds that rolled over the city seemed fitting for this sorrowful day. Whitman scrawled an impression in his notebook: "Lincoln's death—black, black, black—as you look toward the sky—long broad black like great serpents."

Throughout the war, he had expressed strong emotions in his poetry. The poems in *Drum-Taps* were filled with his grief at the death of so many men, his love for the soldiers he nursed, and his concern for their families. Now he used poetry to convey his grief over Lincoln's death.

Whitman recalled the many times he had seen the president on

President Lincoln's funeral procession in Washington, D.C.

Washington's broad avenues. Then, he had compared Lincoln to the captain of a ship. The war had been a treacherous voyage. Now the nation rejoiced that the journey was safely over, but the people had to celebrate without their chief officer.

The poet used this seafaring imagery in one of his best-known works, a poem in memory of Lincoln titled "O Captain! My Captain!" In this poem, a crewmember calls to the captain of his ship, "our fearful trip is done, / The ship has weather'd every rack, the prize we sought is won." Then, a shocking sight stops the speaker's words.

> *But O heart! heart! heart!*
> *O the bleeding drops of red,*
> *Where on the deck my Captain lies,*
> *Fallen cold and dead.*

People who learn bad news commonly feel a sensation of unreality. They may think for a moment that there has been a mistake, or that they will wake up and everything will be as it was. The crewmember in Whitman's poem has this experience. As a crowd on the shore greets the ship with bells, bugle trills, and bouquets, he hopes the dead captain was only a vision from a dream. The captain's pale lips and lack of pulse, however, soon confirm the truth. The speaker is condemned to "Walk the deck my Captain lies, / Fallen cold and dead."

"O Captain! My Captain!" was an unusual poem for Whitman. Its lines rhymed and followed a consistent meter, or rhythm. Later, it would annoy him that many readers preferred this poem to his freer, more experimental works. "I'm almost sorry I ever wrote the poem," he would tell a friend.

So many memories crowded Whitman's mind in the weeks after Lincoln's death. He thought about the lilacs, the spring birds, Venus in the sky—images that reminded him of the last days of Lincoln's life. He wove those images into a great poem of lamentation. Whitman wrote:

When lilacs last in the dooryard bloom'd,
And the great star early droop'd in the western sky in the night,
I mourn'd, and yet shall mourn with ever-returning spring.

Whitman ignored the sprightly, social spring birds and wrote in his poem about the hermit thrush, the bird he learned about from John Burroughs. The thrush, too, mourned. It sang a "Song of the bleeding throat," Whitman said, "Death's outlet song of life."

The poet wondered how he could pay tribute to the great man who died. He asked:

O how shall I warble myself for the dead one there I loved?
And how shall I deck my song for the large sweet soul that has
*   gone?*
And what shall my perfume be for the grave of him I love?
. . . .
And what shall the pictures be that I hang on the walls,
To adorn the burial-house of him I love?

He concluded that the nation itself, whole and at peace, was the greatest possible tribute. He envisioned winds from the Atlantic and Pacific oceans combining with his own breath to perfume the grave. Views of farms, rivers, and cities would adorn an imaginary tomb. There would be pictures of Manhattan and the prairies, and men and women at their labors.

The hermit thrush's song reminded Whitman that death is universal. "In the day, in the night, to all, to each," comes "Sooner or later delicate death."

In his mind, Whitman could see the many soldiers who died in the Civil War:

I saw battle-corpses, myriads of them,
And the white skeletons of young men, I saw them,
I saw the debris and debris of all the slain soldiers of the war . . .

He realized the soldiers were at peace, and took comfort in that knowledge. "They themselves were fully at rest, they suffer'd not."

Whitman ended the poem with a vow to keep alive his memory of the man who died. It is a memory forever linked to the images of early spring.

> *For the sweetest, wisest soul of all my days and lands—and*
> *this for his dear sake,*
> *Lilac and star and bird twined with the chant of my soul . . .*

The thin volume *Drum-Taps* was already being printed. A few copies had even been bound inside their covers. But Whitman stopped the presses without hesitation. Any book of Civil War poetry would be incomplete, he knew, without some lines honoring Lincoln. He added "O Captain! My Captain!" and "When Lilacs Last in the Dooryard Bloom'd," plus two short poems to the book.

Walt Whitman was no longer an unknown poet. A growing number of people heard of *Leaves of Grass* during the 1860s. Many condemned it as scandalous, whether they had read it or not. In June 1865, the secretary of the interior, James Harlan, found a copy of *Leaves of Grass* in Whitman's desk at work. Harlan said he would not have the author of "that book" employed in his department. He issued an announcement stating, "The services of Walter Whitman of New York as a clerk in the Indian Office will be dispensed with from and after this date."

Unexpectedly fired, Whitman soon found another job, working in the attorney general's office. He felt less angry about being let go than about Harlan searching his desk. A man like Harlan could never understand the importance of *Leaves of Grass*, Whitman knew. As he explained, "He was only a fool: there was only a dim light in his noddle: he had to steer by that light: what else could he do?"

But the poet's friends were outraged. William O'Connor wrote a fifteen-page letter of protest to Harlan, reminding the secretary of Whitman's work in the hospitals and praising *Leaves of Grass*. O'Con-

O the bleeding drops of red!

O CAPTAIN! MY CAPTAIN!

BY WALT WHITMAN.

I.

O CAPTAIN! my captain! our fearful trip is done
The ship has weathered every rack, the prize we sought is won;
The port is near, the bells I hear, the people all exulting,
While follow eyes the steady keel, the vessel grim and daring.
But O heart! heart! heart!
~~Leave you not the little spot~~
Where on the deck my captain lies,
Fallen cold and dead.

II.

O captain! my captain! rise up and hear the bells;
Rise up! for you the flag is flung, for you the bugle trills:
For you bouquets and ribboned wreaths, for you the shores a-crowd-
ing:
For you they call, the swaying mass, their eager faces turning.
O captain! dear father!
This arm ~~I push beneath you.~~ *beneath your head;*
It is some dream that on the deck
You've fallen cold and dead.

III.

My captain does not answer, his lips are pale and still:
My father does not feel my arm, he has no pulse nor will.
~~But the ship,~~ The ship is anchored safe, its voyage closed and done: *and*
From fearful trip the victor ship comes in with object won! *sound.*
Exult, O shores! and ring, O bells!
But I, with silent tread,
Walk the spot my captain lies
Fallen cold and dead.

As this page proof shows, Whitman was still revising his poetry once printing had begun.

nor calmed down and never sent the letter. He kept writing, though, and soon completed a pamphlet, *The Good Gray Poet*, championing Whitman's character and his poetry. John Burroughs set out to improve his friend's reputation by writing a biography of Walt Whitman.

Whitman made a new friend as 1865 came to a close. On a stormy night, he boarded a car of Washington's street railway. He had wrapped a blanket around his shoulders to stay warm, and the railway conductor, a young man named Peter Doyle, thought he looked like an old sea captain. Doyle took a seat next to Walt—the sole passenger—and started a conversation. Enjoying himself, Walt rode to the end of the railway line with Doyle, and then back.

On the nights that followed, Walt often rode the railway with Pete Doyle and then joined him for a drink after work. He and Pete took long walks through the city, and Walt at last began to feel strong and well again. He whistled and sang, he recited poetry, and he lectured to his young friend on geography and astronomy. "Walt knew all about the stars," Pete said. "He was eloquent when he talked about them."

Washington's street railway.

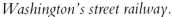

Whitman and Peter Doyle.

The next summer, Whitman traveled to New York to watch over the printing of a new edition of *Leaves of Grass*. He wrote to John Burroughs, "if it wasn't for the worriment of the book, I should be as happy as a clam at high water, as they say down on old Long Island."

Whitman's poems were gaining readers both in the United States and in Europe. After the firm of Thayer and Eldridge folded, however, no other publishing company wanted to print *Leaves of Grass*. Whitman had gone back to publishing the book himself. He sold the copies by mail for three dollars each.

Sometimes readers wrote to Whitman to say they admired him and his work. Many women were attracted to him as his fame grew. They did not mind that, at fifty-one, his long white hair made him look like an old man. One lovesick woman handed him a rose as he rode the street railway.

In 1871, Walt received the first of many letters from an English-woman, a widow named Anne Gilchrist. She wrote that Whitman's poems had taught her a great deal. "I never before dreamed what love meant," she said, "Never was alive before." The beauty of Whitman's poetry had stirred feelings of affection in Gilchrist. She said Whitman made "each reader feel that he himself or herself has an actual relationship to him." She admitted that she loved the poet, although they had never met.

Walt responded politely to Anne Gilchrist, addressing her as "Dear Friend." He warned her, "The actual W. W. is a very plain personage, and entirely unworthy such devotion."

It was new works, and not love, that now attracted Whitman. He wrote a booklet, *Democratic Vistas*, in support of democracy and the right to vote. Democracy bound "all nations, all men, of however various and distant lands, into a brotherhood, a family," Whitman wrote. But democracy in the United States was threatened by corruption, Whitman feared, by "the depravity of the business classes." A desire to live the "fashionable life" diverted people from the honesty and heroism that had built America and would keep the nation strong.

Anne Gilchrist.

Whitman sent this picture of himself to Anne Gilchrist.

Whitman embarked on a new journey in his poetry when he wrote "Passage to India." Until now, *Leaves of Grass* contained "the songs of Body and Existence," Whitman explained. This new poem would sing about "spiritual law."

Centuries earlier, Christopher Columbus had traveled unknown waters, looking for a new route to India. Instead of reaching India, he landed in the New World. Whitman wanted to take a "Passage to more than India!" to explore the unknown territory of the human spirit. He hoped to resolve questions that have perplexed humanity since the beginning of history. For example, people have long asked, what is the meaning of life? And, how is peace of mind achieved? As Whitman put it:

> *Adam and Eve appear, then their myriad progeny after them,*
> *Wandering, yearning, curious, with restless explorations,*
> *With questionings, baffled, formless, feverish, with never-happy*
>   *hearts,*
> *With that sad incessant refrain,* Wherefore unsatisfied soul? *and*
>   Whither O mocking life?

Whitman asked,

> *Ah who shall soothe these feverish children?*
> *Who justify these restless explorations?*

The poet would answer the great questions, Whitman stated. In "Passage to India," he looked ahead to the day when he would discover the secrets of the sea, the sunrise, the rain and snow, the moon and stars. Meanwhile, dark clouds were again gathering over his life.

His political discussions with William O'Connor had been growing louder and angrier. Walt had held his temper in check for a long time, but one night, it exploded. He shouted insults at O'Connor, and O'Connor replied with hurtful remarks. Not only was the friendship destroyed that night, but O'Connor walked out on his wife as well. He accused Nelly of taking Whitman's side in the dispute.

And there were more family problems to cloud Whitman's happiness. Jesse had died at the King's County Lunatic Asylum. Walt's sister Hannah was unhappy in her marriage to Charles Heyde. Walt went to see Hannah, who lived in Vermont, in 1872. His visit cheered her greatly, and he promised to come again. This would be the last time, however, that the brother and sister would ever see each other.

Walt also had his mother to worry about. Louisa Whitman had grown too old and frail to care for herself. She gave up her home in Brooklyn. She and Eddy went to Camden, New Jersey, to live with George and his wife. George now worked as an inspector at a Camden pipe factory. It was a difficult move for the aging woman. Walt wrote her an understanding letter. "Mother, it is always disagreeable to make a great change, & especially for old folks," he said.

By January 1873, Louisa Whitman was still adjusting to her new quarters. Walt tried to think of a way to move his mother and Eddy to Washington. On January 23, he worked late in his office. The sky outside was dark. Rain and sleet covered the streets with a layer of slush.

Walt began to feel weary and faint. He stretched out on a sofa in front of a fireplace to do some reading. Soon, he grew too weak to hold his book. A building guard noticed that Whitman looked ill and volunteered to help him get home. Walt thanked the man but said he could manage alone.

Once back in his own room, Walt went straight to bed and quickly fell asleep. He awoke in the middle of the night to discover that the left side of his body was numb. He could not move his left arm or leg.

A doctor examined Walt in the morning. The doctor made a diagnosis: The patient had had an attack of "left hemiplagia." Today, physicians would say Walt Whitman had suffered a stroke.

CHAPTER NINE

Backward Glances

My Book and I—what a period we have presumed to span! those thirty years from 1850 to '80—and America in them!

T HE NINETEENTH-CENTURY phrenologists taught that each section of the brain controlled a personality trait. Scientists now know that particular areas of the brain control such functions as speech, thought, and movement. Every part of the brain needs a steady supply of blood, rich in oxygen and nutrients, to carry out its tasks.

When a stroke occurs, part of the brain's blood supply is cut off. A vessel may be blocked, or it may have burst. Starved for blood, brain tissue dies. Some functioning may be lost, depending on the part of the brain affected. If a stroke is severe enough, a person can die.

Walt Whitman's stroke left him able to think and to speak, but he had to learn to walk all over again. It was hard work. He was so weak at first that walking ten steps made him tired and sick. He often sat in a rocking chair while his friends cared for him. John Burroughs was in New York at this time, so his wife, Ursula, took turns with Nelly O'Connor, Charles Eldridge, and Peter Doyle to make Whitman's bed and clean his room. The friends picked up his medicines at the pharmacy.

By the middle of February, Whitman could take short walks in the street if his friends supported him. In May, he went back to work for a few hours each day, walking with a cane.

That same month, he received word that his mother, too, was ill. Walt traveled to Camden as soon as he could, arriving on May 20. Louisa Whitman died three days later.

The loss of his mother was "the great dark cloud of my life," Whitman said. "My physical sickness, bad as it is, is nothing to it." Too upset to sleep, he spent the night before the funeral sitting beside his mother's coffin. He tapped out a mournful rhythm on the hard floor with his cane.

Unfit now to work at all, Whitman made a quick trip to Washington to arrange a leave of absence from his job. He saw Charles Eldridge, who was alarmed at his appearance. Whitman seemed to be "in a very depressed condition," Eldridge told John Burroughs. "I begin to wonder whether Walt is going to recover . . ."

Walt was desperate for any reminder of his mother. Back in Camden, he slept in her room at George's house and sat in her favorite chair. "Every object of furniture, &c. is familiar & has an emotional history," he wrote. He treasured the small scrap of paper that held his mother's last written words: "dont mourn for me my beloved sons and daughters. farewell my dear beloved walter."

In a happier moment, Walt Whitman had compared himself to Christopher Columbus, sailing uncharted seas and discovering new worlds. Now he wrote a poem titled "Prayer of Columbus" that described the famous explorer as "A batter'd, wreck'd old man . . ." Friends who read the poem thought Whitman was really describing himself. "I am too full of woe!" Columbus says in the poem. "Haply I may not live another day."

It is no wonder that Whitman felt so discouraged. A ferry ride across the Delaware River, from Camden to Philadelphia, left him dizzy and tired. He was invited to Tufts College near Boston to recite a poem at the graduation ceremony, but he was too weak to make the trip. With only six hundred dollars to his name, he was "ridiculously poor," he said. Then in July 1874, the government informed him that his job was being given to someone else. Walt realized he would have to remain in Camden with George and his wife, who was named Louisa like his mother.

Walt felt so depressed that he often sat alone for hours doing nothing. It seemed impossible that things could get worse. But in February 1875, he had another stroke, one that affected the right side of his body. Thinking back on this time, Whitman later said, "I was down, down, down that year. I came out of it—God knows how."

Two medicines always lifted Whitman's spirits—poetry and friendship. They helped him now. He produced a two-volume edition of his work in 1876, honoring the one-hundredth birthday of the United States. The "Centennial Edition" of *Leaves of Grass* contained "Passage to India" and other new writings. Still acting as his own publisher and mail-order house, Whitman sold the set for ten dollars.

By now Whitman had recovered enough to get out and walk again. He befriended an eighteen-year-old errand boy named Harry Stafford. Harry introduced Walt to his parents, George and Susan Stafford, who were farmers. Whitman was always at ease among working people, and the Staffords took to him right away. "I think he is the best man I ever knew," said Susan Stafford.

Soon Walt was staying for weeks at a time at the Stafford farm, where he was treated as one of the family. "Am with folks I love and that love me," he wrote in his notebook. He thrived on Susan Stafford's plain country cooking, finishing hearty plates of eggs, roasted chicken, and freshly butchered pork. On cool evenings, he sat with the family in front of a crackling fire. He credited the Staffords with saving his life. "If I had not known you," he confided to Harry Stafford, "I should not be a living man to-day."

The Staffords lived near a wooded stream called Timber Creek. On pleasant days, Whitman followed a path to the water. He leaned on his cane as he walked, and he dragged his left foot, which would always be lame. Whitman had felt close to nature many years earlier, as a child on Long Island. Now his love of the outdoors returned. Timber Creek was a private world of trees and running water, soft grass and sunny skies. It was a world of "sane, silent, beauteous miracles," Whitman said.

Sometimes he stripped naked to bathe in the creek or wade in the mud. As if testing his strength, he wrestled with pliant saplings. He imagined the life and energy of the young trees entering his body like "health's wine," he said, nourishing him from head to toe. He was once again like the child who went forth every day. He observed nature closely, using all five senses. Like Thoreau at Walden Pond, he wrote prose descriptions of the small miracles he witnessed.

May, he wrote, was "the bumble-bee month." The hundreds of bees that droned past him were "big fellows with light yellow jackets," Whitman noted, "great glistening swelling bodies, stumpy heads and gauzy wings—humming their perpetual rich mellow boom."

As spring passed into summer, Whitman took notice of "the white and pink pond-blossoms, with great heart-shaped leaves; the glassy waters of the creek, the banks, with dense bushery, and the picturesque beeches and shade and turf; the tremulous, reedy call of some bird from recesses, breaking the warm, indolent, half voluptuous silence." Sitting on a tree stump, Whitman watched the dragonflies that hovered over the creek, "circling and darting and occasionally balancing themselves quite still, their wings quivering all the time."

"How it all nourishes, lulls me, in the way most needed," he concluded, "the open air, the rye fields, the apple orchards."

In 1876, Anne Gilchrist and her children moved from England to Philadelphia. Gilchrist wanted to be close to Walt, and she dreamed that they might marry. "O I passionately believe there are years in store for us, years of tranquil, tender happiness," she wrote to the man she loved.

Many times, Walt Whitman rode the ferry from Camden to Philadelphia and visited the Gilchrist home. He had his own room there, and Anne liked to hear him singing before breakfast. The songs were "an outburst of pure emotional and physical *abandon* to the delight of living," she believed. The Gilchrists carried Walt's chair outdoors when it was warm so he could chat with passing neighbors.

It pleased Whitman's old friends to see a change in his appearance. "Never saw Walt look so handsome, so new and fresh," John Burroughs commented.

Another source of happiness in Whitman's life was the birth of a nephew, a child George and Louisa named after his uncle Walter. Through the spring of 1877, Walt played with the infant and helped to care for him. But soon he was sitting beside a coffin once more. The baby had died during a summer heat wave.

Stricken with grief himself, Whitman tried to comfort the children who paid their respects to his dead nephew. He asked one little girl who peered into the coffin, "You don't understand this, my dear, do you?" The girl replied that she did not. "Neither do I," Whitman told her.

As a beginning poet, Walt Whitman had preached that death was a passage from one form of life to another. Death was as joyous as birth, he said at that time. Then Whitman saw death firsthand. He watched soldiers die in hospitals. He mourned a beloved president. In a few short years, he lost two brothers, his mother, and his cherished nephew. Whitman found no joy in these deaths. He found only suffering.

The years brought many changes. Harry Stafford married. Walt saw less of his young friend, who was now busy with a new life. In 1879, Anne Gilchrist came to understand that she and Whitman would never marry. Whitman always treated her kindly, but she could see that he did not return her love. She and her family sailed back to England.

Walt, too, did some traveling in that year. In February, he went to New York to give a lecture on Abraham Lincoln. The audience loved to hear him describe seeing Lincoln in Manhattan in 1861. They were moved at his recital of "When Lilacs Last in the Dooryard Bloom'd." Whitman would repeat this popular lecture often for the rest of his life.

In 1879, Whitman took his first and only trip west, going by train from Philadelphia to Denver, Colorado, and into the Rocky Mountains. He used red ink to mark his route on a map of the United States, and he wrote to Anne Gilchrist that he was at last seeing *"the real America."*

Whitman fell in love with Denver right away, he said. It was a city

A passenger train snakes through the Rocky Mountains in the 1880s.

of clean air and rugged miners. From Denver, at one mile above sea level, he looked east over miles of prairie. When he turned toward the west, he saw mountains rising into a "violet haze."

The trip through the Rockies was thrilling, Whitman wrote, whether the train went "squirming around corners, or up and down hills." The train sped past streams, chasms, and towering peaks—scenes of pure nature, untouched by civilization. Whitman felt that, at last, "I have found the law of my own poems." He had always tried to write poems that were as pure as nature. He had tried to present authentic thoughts and observations that were unmarred by such trappings as long words, tricky rhymes, and fancy figures of speech.

Whitman stopped in St. Louis, where his brother Jeff had settled. He spent the summer of 1880 in Canada, and paid a visit to Dr. Richard Maurice Bucke, an admirer of his work.

Whitman posed with Harry and Kitty Johnston, two young friends, in 1879.

Bucke was the director of a mental hospital in Ontario. He invited Whitman to tour the institution, and he soon came upon his guest using the hospital library. Bucke saw that Whitman had a dozen or more open books spread across the table in front of him. Whitman was scanning their pages for facts, in the same way that he had soaked up knowledge in the years before writing his first great poems.

In 1881, Walt Whitman went to Boston for the printing of a new edition of *Leaves of Grass*. James R. Osgood and Company had offered to publish the book. A few weeks after the book was printed, however, the Boston district attorney informed the publisher that *Leaves of Grass* violated the city's obscenity laws. Several passages had to be omitted.

It would be impossible for Whitman to leave out any lines and remain true to himself, he told his publisher. "I know I am restless and make others so," he later explained. "For I confront peace, security, and all the settled laws, to unsettle them." James R. Osgood and Company had no choice but to stop publication of the book.

Whitman was about to print the new edition himself, as he had in the past, when a Philadelphia publisher asked to take on the job. The new company printed three thousand copies of *Leaves of Grass* and sold them all in one day.

As *Leaves of Grass* gained readers, the plan for a new book took shape in Whitman's mind: Why not put his memories down on paper and gather them in a book? This new work would be "the most wayward, spontaneous, fragmentary book ever printed," Whitman knew. It would be, he said, "a rapid skimming over the pond-surface of my life, thoughts, experiences . . ."

Walt Whitman was now sixty-three years old. The journey of life had taken him from the beaches of Long Island to the streets of Manhattan and into the hospitals of the Civil War. He had immersed himself in nature at Timber Creek and had traveled west. He included all of those events in the new book, titled *Specimen Days*.

He described in *Specimen Days* how his viewpoint had changed as he approached old age. He said that as a younger man, he strove to write poems that were "charged with sunshine." Now, he wrote, "as

I grow old, the half-lights of evening are far more to me." No longer did he write long, expansive poems like "Song of Myself." He wrote brief poems now, word sketches of sunsets, winter sounds, and images of death. His great work was done.

In 1881, the Whitmans placed Eddy in an institution. Three years later, George and Louisa Whitman moved to Burlington, New Jersey. They asked Walt to come with them, but he declined to go. George expressed disappointment, but Walt believed his decision was for the best. His habits had always conflicted with his sister-in-law's housekeeping schedule. For example, it bothered her greatly that Walt still would not eat dinner with the rest of the family. Now, Walt took his bath while the others ate. And he never bathed quietly. He sang loudly in the tub, choosing patriotic songs such as, "The Star-Spangled Banner," or Civil War tunes such as, "When Johnny Comes Marching Home."

Walt had earned enough money from his books and lectures to buy a small house for himself. The house was on Mickle Street, in a noisy section of Camden. The clatter of passing trains, whistles from

Whitman's house on Mickle Street.

nearby factories, and the clashing notes of a neighbor's piano reached his ears even with the windows closed. But lilac bushes grew in the yard, and these gave Whitman peace.

Declining health made it hard for Whitman to get around. His dizzy spells had returned, his vision was often blurred, and he had grown more lame. He kept to a single upstairs room, where he cooked on a kerosene stove. He used a packing crate for a dining table and drank water out of a pitcher. Most of the house was empty of furniture.

Whitman spent his time tidying up the loose fragments of his life. He sorted through the thousands of papers he had saved over the years—bits of poetry, old letters, and souvenirs. He still had the letter Emerson wrote to him so many years earlier. He treasured his mother's last written words. Some papers he kept, and others he burned. Those were "too sacred," he said, "too surely and only mine" for others to read after his death.

An artist's drawing of the interior of Whitman's bedroom.

A page of Whitman's commonplace book from 1881. For much of his life, the poet recorded day-to-day events in notebooks such as this.

The Eagle Street College, a group of Whitman's English admirers.

Walt Whitman's fame was growing, and many people who had read *Leaves of Grass* came to see him in Camden. Artists arrived to paint his portrait or photograph him. The Irish writer Oscar Wilde drank punch with Whitman while on a visit to the United States. A young man named Horace Traubel often came over to talk about literature with the poet he revered.

After years of neglect, Whitman relished the attention. Happy in the role of "good gray poet," he welcomed all of his guests. He answered letters from American and European readers. At times, he tried to create myths about himself. He told some people, for example, that he was the father of several sons and daughters. "Tho' always unmarried I have had six children," he wrote to an English correspondent. There is no evidence that these children existed, or

Many people found Whitman's appearance in old age to be striking.

that Whitman ever had a relationship with a woman who could have been their mother.

Visitors to the Mickle Street house saw a white-haired man with a long beard who wore his hat indoors. Six feet tall and weighing two hundred pounds, Whitman still appeared striking. "Never has such a beautiful old man appeared among men," said a young poet who traveled to Camden. If guests commented on the confusion of papers that spilled from his old trunk and covered the floor, Whitman told them, "This is not so much of a mess as it looks." He pointed out that "I find most of the things I look for, and without much trouble."

But it disturbed Whitman's fans to see the way he lived. Worried about his income, they sent him gifts of money. Whitman looked poorer than he was. He used much of the donated money to build himself a tomb in Camden's Harleigh Cemetery.

In 1885, a group of admirers gave ten dollars apiece to buy a horse and buggy for Whitman, so that he could ride outdoors each day. Some contributed because they appreciated Whitman's poetry, others because they remembered his selfless work during the Civil War. Whitman's verses were "among the most cynical instances of indecent exposure I recollect," said the Boston writer Oliver Wendell Holmes. But Holmes added, "he served well the cause of humanity and I do not begrudge him a ten dollar bill."

Whitman received the buggy with tears in his eyes. He would use it to take many rides through the streets of Camden, alone or with friends. Each day, he rode to the cemetery to visit the graves of his mother and his nephew Walt.

John Burroughs came to see Whitman two weeks after the new carriage arrived. "Walt drives me to the station with his new horse and buggy—the first time I ever saw him drive," Burroughs stated. Burroughs worried, though, that his old friend was neglecting his health. "Walt eats very heartily—too heartily, I think, and tell him so," Burroughs said.

His friends may have wanted Walt Whitman to live on forever,

Walt Whitman, an old man, photographed by the artist Thomas Eakins.

Whitman riding in his buggy with a young neighbor.

but the poet knew the end of his life was near. When he prepared *November Boughs*, a small book of his later poems, in 1888, he composed a long preface in which he looked back on his years as a writer.

"So here I sit gossiping in the early candlelight of old age—I and my book—casting backward glances over our travel'd road," he wrote. Whitman weighed the success of his literary journey, and "from a worldly and business point of view 'Leaves of Grass' has been worse than a failure," he conceded. But making money had never been his goal. He had wanted to capture his personality and nineteenth-century America in words. He had tried to create a new kind of poetry for the United States. Achieving those goals had been an adventure.

"My Book and I," he wrote in *November Boughs*, "what a period we have presumed to span! those thirty years from 1850 to '80—and America in them! Proud, proud indeed may we be, if we have cull'd enough of that period in its own spirit to worthily waft a few live breaths of it to the future!"

Walt Whitman, looking frail and ill, surrounded by his papers and mementos.

CHAPTER TEN

Nightfall

The strongest and sweetest songs yet remain to be sung.

WALT WHITMAN SAW the first printed pages of *November Boughs* on his sixty-ninth birthday. "It's my baby book just born today," he told the friends who gathered to have dinner with him. "Don't you see? I am celebrating two birthdays today."

The party guests toasted Whitman's health. But three days later, a series of strokes brought the poet to the floor of his bedroom. The new strokes left Whitman sluggish and sometimes confused. He had more trouble walking than before. Whitman believed he was about to die, and so did his friends. "I think he has in his own mind given up the fight and awaits the end," John Burroughs wrote in his diary. Burroughs and Horace Traubel made plans for Whitman's funeral.

Whitman lived on, though, for nearly four years. No longer able to drive his buggy, he got around in a wheelchair. Neighbors took him to the cemetery, where he supervised the construction of his tomb. It was to be a "plain massive stone temple," he said, built into a tree-topped hillside. With only the name WALT WHITMAN carved over the door, the tomb had burial space for eight people. "It is my design to gather the remains of our dear father and mother and have them buried here in the tomb I have built for myself," Whitman wrote to his sister Hannah.

He lived long enough to finish another project, the one that had

Whitman seated beside an open window.

been his life's occupation. In January 1892, he sent this notice to the *New York Herald*:

> Walt Whitman wishes respectfully to notify the public that the book *Leaves of Grass*, which he has been working on at great intervals and partially issued for the past thirty-five or forty years, is now completed, so to call it, and he would like this new 1892 edition to absolutely supersede all previous ones. Faulty as it is, he decides it as by far his special and entire self-chosen poetic utterance.

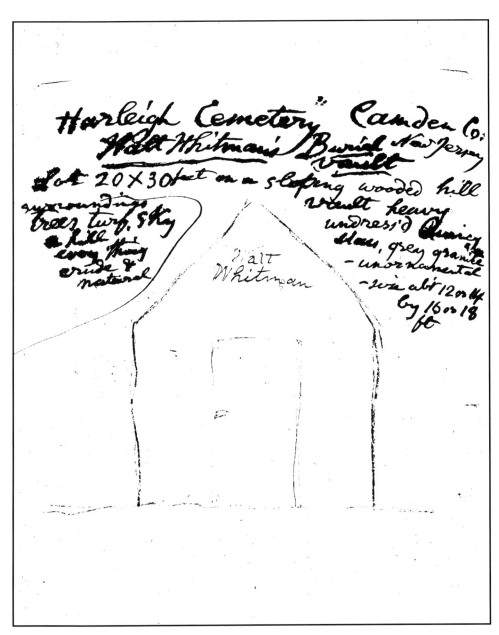

The poet's sketch for his tomb.

There would be no more new poems, no more revisions.

The final, or "Death-Bed," edition of *Leaves of Grass* contained 438 pages that were crammed with print. "Crossing Brooklyn Ferry," "Song of Myself," "The Wound-Dresser," "O Captain! My Captain!"—the 389 poems sang about the author's life and times. They rang with the sound of boots on city sidewalks and the voices of people in the streets.

Within the spreading lines, blacksmiths lowered their heavy sledgehammers. Farmers, fishermen, and trappers went about their work. Whitman's verses described soldiers marching or making camp for the night, the beautiful "body electric," naked and free of shame, and the American land and its resources. Whitman's pages sprouted "the grass that grows wherever the land is and the water is."

The pages contained one of the last poems Whitman wrote. "Good-bye My Fancy!" held fond parting words for the imagination that had served him long and well:

> *The slower fainter ticking of the clock is in me,*
> *Exit, nightfall, and soon the heart-thud stopping.*
>
> *Long have we lived, joy'd, caress'd together;*
> *Delightful!—now separation—Good-bye my Fancy.*

Walt Whitman's work was done. On March 17, he thought of Hannah once more. He sent her a last note and a small gift of money. "Unable to write much," he scribbled, "God bless you—WW." On the evening of March 26, 1892, Whitman's lungs failed, and he died.

Men and women filled Mickle Street on March 30, the day of the poet's funeral. Peter Doyle, just in from Washington, had trouble getting through the crowd and into Whitman's house! The many mourners waited a long time to file past the coffin. Some had known Whitman personally, while others had come to know him only through his poems.

During the funeral service, friends and admirers of Whitman read from books of religion and philosophy, such as the teachings of

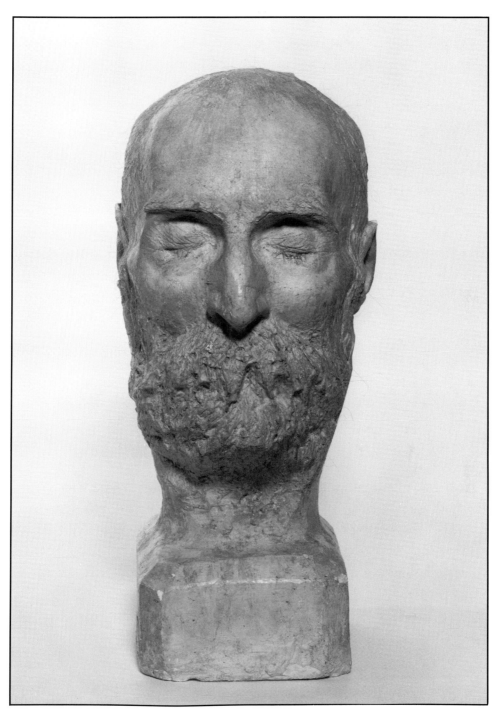

A death mask of Whitman by Thomas Eakins.

Buddha and Confucius, the Koran, and the Bible. Some read passages from Whitman's "new Bible," *Leaves of Grass*. Then Walt Whitman, who had once promised to sprout again from the earth, was laid to rest in his tomb.

Whitman had been a devoted son and brother throughout his life. He had always looked after those he loved. That concern for his family extended beyond his death. The bodies of his parents were moved to his tomb, as he had wished. In time, the tomb would also shelter the remains of Hannah, Eddy, George and his wife, Louisa, and the infant Walt.

Whitman's tomb in Camden, New Jersey.

In his will, Whitman specified that most of his money and the future profits from *Leaves of Grass* be used to pay for Eddy's care. He left a small sum to Nancy Whitman, the widow of his alcoholic brother Andrew. Peter Doyle and Harry Stafford, young friends who had brought joy into Whitman's life, each received one of his watches. Walt Whitman's greatest legacy, however, was *Leaves of Grass*, the book he left to the world.

In the 1860 edition of *Leaves of Grass*, Whitman first published a poem called "Starting from Paumanok." In this poem, he saw for himself "an audience interminable," a never-ending army of readers in the centuries to come. He wrote:

> *With firm and regular step they wend, they never stop,*
> *Successions of men, Americanos, a hundred millions,*
> *One generation playing its part and passing on,*
> *Another generation playing its part and passing on in its turn,*
> *With faces turn'd sideways or backward towards me to listen,*
> *With eyes retrospective towards me.*

Whitman often thought, too, about the poets of future generations. Those men and women would continue the tradition of new American poetry that he had only begun. "The strongest and sweetest songs yet remain to be sung," Whitman optimistically declared in 1888.

A new century arrived less than a decade after Whitman's death. The twentieth century brought technological advances that nineteenth-century people never could have imagined. Henry Ford founded the Ford Motor Company in 1903. Soon, highways cut into the landscape and Americans commonly traveled between cities by automobile. It was in 1903, too, that the Wright brothers made the first airplane flight. Jet aircraft began carrying passengers in the 1950s. And by the end of the century, astronauts were conducting scientific experiments in space. Technology brought advances in communication, including the television and the computer.

Twentieth-century Americans fought wars in Europe, Africa, and Asia. The Great Depression of the 1930s disrupted the lives of most citizens. During the twentieth century, African Americans and other minority groups worked to secure their rights and gain opportunities.

New generations of poets have described the sights, sounds, and emotions of twentieth-century life. Many have acknowledged their debt to Walt Whitman as they have continued the chronicle of America. Hart Crane (1899–1932) wrote a book of poetry, *The Bridge*, inspired by the Brooklyn Bridge. This bridge was a great technological achievement when it was completed in 1883. It linked Brooklyn and Manhattan. Bridge crossers made the same trip that Whitman had so often taken by ferry.

Gulls glided in the sky over the bridge Crane described, just as they circled above Whitman's ferry. Crane wrote:

> *The seagull's wings shall dip and pivot him,*
> *Shedding white rings of tumult, building high*
> *Over the chained bay waters Liberty—*

Langston Hughes (1902–1967) wrote about African-American life. Like Whitman, he described ordinary men, women, and children. At times he created long, repetitious lines of poetry that were similar to the ones Whitman pioneered. These verses are from the Hughes poem "The Negro Speaks of Rivers":

> *I built my hut near the Congo and it lulled me*
> *   to sleep.*
> *I looked upon the Nile and raised the pyramids*
> *   above it.*
> *I heard the singing of the Mississippi when Abe Lincoln*
> *   went down to New Orleans, and I've seen its muddy*
> *   bosom turn all golden in the sunset.*

The contemporary poet Allen Ginsberg often describes the American scene in his work. Like Whitman, he frequently creates lengthy,

*A Boston bookstore displayed a collection of Whitman's books, letters, and
photographs at the turn of the century.*

chanting lines. Ginsberg spoke about Whitman's writing style in a television program on the great poet. "Whitman opened up space completely, opened up the space of the line, broke open the line, so he could say anything he wanted," Ginsberg said. The long lines gave Whitman room to mention many details of everyday life, Ginsberg explained.

"The longer the line, the more music can build up," added another poet interviewed for the program, Galway Kinnell.

In the musical lines of "Song of Myself," Whitman foresaw himself taking a "perpetual journey" with future readers:

> *No friend of mine takes his ease in my chair . . .*
> *. . . . .*
> *But each man and each woman of you I lead upon a knoll,*
> *My left hand hooking you round the waist,*
> *My right hand pointing to landscapes of continents and*
>   *the public road.*

The world is about to enter a new century, one that promises further discoveries and change. And still Walt Whitman invites poets and readers to come on the journey he started in 1855. "Shoulder your duds dear son, and I will mine, and let us hasten forth," he beckons in "Song of Myself," "Wonderful cities and free nations we shall fetch as we go."

Selected Bibliography

Chase, Richard. *Walt Whitman*. Minneapolis: University of Minnesota, 1961.

Kaplan, Justin. *Walt Whitman: A Life*. New York: Simon and Schuster, 1980.

Kimmel, Stanley. *Mr. Lincoln's Washington*. New York: Coward-McCann, Inc., 1957.

Kunhardt, Philip B., Jr., Philip B. Kunhardt III, and Peter W. Kunhardt. *Lincoln: An Illustrated Biography*. New York: Alfred A. Knopf, 1992.

Leech, Margaret. *Reveille in Washington: 1860-1865*. Alexandria, Va.: Time-Life Books, 1962.

McPherson, James M. *Ordeal By Fire (Volume II: The Civil War)*. New York: Alfred A. Knopf, 1982.

Reynolds, David S. "Of Me I Sing: Whitman in His Time." *The New York Times Book Review*, October 4, 1992.

Simon, Kate. *Fifth Avenue: A Very Social History*. New York: Harcourt Brace Jovanovich, 1978.

Stokesbury, James L. *A Short History of the American Revolution*. New York: William Morrow and Company, 1991.

Trager, James. *West of Fifth: The Rise and Fall and Rise of Manhattan's West Side*. New York: Atheneum, 1987.

Van Doren, Mark, ed. *The Portable Walt Whitman*. New York: The Viking Press, 1973. (This book contains selections from *Leaves of Grass* and the complete text of *Democratic Vistas* and *Specimen Days*.)

Vendler, Helen, ed. *Voices and Visions: The Poet in America*. New York: Random House, 1987.

Voices and Visions, Episode 12. The Annenberg/CPB Collection. Producer: New York Center for Visual History, 1988.

Whitman, Walt. *Leaves of Grass*. New York: W. W. Norton & Company, 1973.

————. *Walt Whitman's Civil War*. New York: Alfred A. Knopf, 1960.

Winwar, Frances. *American Giant: Walt Whitman and His Times*. New York: Tudor Publishing Company, 1941.

Zweig, Paul. *Walt Whitman: The Making of the Poet*. New York: Basic Books, 1984.

Picture Credits

❦

The Charles E. Feinberg Collection, The Library of Congress: frontispiece, 6, 9, 36, 39, 40, 48, 51, 60, 64, 87, 88, 89, 92, 103, 105, 107, 117, 119, 120, 121, 122, 123, 128, 130, 131, 134, 137

The Library of Congress: 3, 16, 18, 20, 21, 23, 29, 30, 34, 38, 42, 44, 45, 56, 57, 73, 77, 79, 80, 81, 84, 91, 94, 99, 104

Courtesy of the Bayley-Whitman Collection, Ohio Wesleyan University: 9

The Huntington Historical Society: 11, 24

The Brooklyn Historical Society: 14, 40

Brown Brothers: 27

The Metropolitan Museum of Art, New York, Gift of Mr. and Mrs. Carl Stoeckel. 1897 (97.5): 63

Courtesy of the Bostonian Society/Old State House: 66

Harvard Theatre Collection: 72

Burton Historical Collection, The Detroit Public Library: 74

The Trent Collection, Special Collections Library, Duke University: 77

The Beinecke Rare Book and Manuscript Library, Yale University: 108, 125, 126

Denver Public Library, Western History Department: 116

By permission of the Houghton Library, Harvard University (Z Closet): 133

Index

Numbers in *italics* indicate illustrations.

About the Author

❧

"Again and again, while researching books I was writing, I kept bumping into Walt Whitman," says Catherine Reef. "Whether the topic was the Civil War, the life of Thoreau, or the coming of railroads to the West, Whitman was there, singing with words. I realized that his was a story worth telling."

The author of more than twenty nonfiction books for young people, Catherine Reef grew up in Commack, New York—one of the towns where Walt Whitman delivered newspapers in the 1830s. She received her B.A. in English from Washington State University, and lives in Montgomery Village, Maryland, with her husband, her teenage son, their dog, and five tanks of tropical fish. *Walt Whitman* is her first book for Clarion.